Women of Achievement

Rachael Ray

Women of Achievement

Susan B. Anthony

Hillary Rodham Clinton

Marie Curie

Ellen DeGeneres

Nancy Pelosi

Rachael Ray

Eleanor Roosevelt

Martha Stewart

Women of Achievement

Rachael Ray

FOOD ENTREPRENEUR

Dennis Abrams

CHELSEA HOUSE
PUBLISHERS
An imprint of Infobase Publishing

RACHAEL RAY

Chelsea House
An imprint of Infobase Publishing
132 West 31st Street
New York NY 10001

Library of Congress Cataloging-in-Publication Data
Abrams, Dennis, 1960-
  Rachael Ray : Food Entrepreneur / Dennis Abrams.
      p. cm. — (Women of achievement)
  Includes bibliographical references and index.
  ISBN 978-1-60413-078-2 (hardcover : alk. paper) 1. Ray, Rachael. 2. Cooks—
United States—Biography. I. Title. II. Series.

  TX649.R235A27 2009
  641.5092—dc22
  [B]

                                    2008034642

Chelsea House books are available at special discounts when purchased in bulk quantities for businesses, associations, institutions, or sales promotions. Please call our Special Sales Department in New York at (212) 967-8800 or (800) 322-8755.

You can find Chelsea House on the World Wide Web at http://www.chelseahouse.com

Series design by Erik Lindstrom
Cover design by Ben Peterson

Printed in the United States of America

EJB Bang 10 9 8 7 6 5 4 3 2

This book is printed on acid-free paper.

All links and Web addresses were checked and verified to be correct at the time of publication. Because of the dynamic nature of the Web, some addresses and links may have changed since publication and may no longer be valid.

CONTENTS

Talking Her Way to the Top

As the fall 2006 television season got under way, four daytime talk shows were waiting to make their debuts. Megan Mullally, the two-time Emmy Award-winning star of the hit television show *Will and Grace*, hoped to have another success with *The Megan Mullally Show*. Greg Behrendt, comic and author of the best-selling books *He's Just Not That Into You* and *It's Called a Break-up Because It's Broken*, premiered *The Greg Behrendt Show*. Psychiatrist Keith Ablow kicked off *The Dr. Keith Ablow Show*. And finally, Food Network star and best-selling cookbook author Rachael Ray jumped into the highly competitive daytime-television arena with her own talk show, called simply *Rachael Ray*.

Variety, considered by most people in the entertainment industry to be *the* show-business bible, had this to say about her debut:

> Known primarily for her thrifty 30-minute meals, Food Network's breakout star Rachael Ray enters daytime TV like a jolt of caffeine to the blood-stream. With an energy level to rival a Jack Russell terrier's, the vivacious chef brings to mind adjectives such as plucky and perky. Her motto is "Can Do!" Her show seemingly could work on that infectious Sicilian gusto alone. . . . A more accessible, less felonious version of Martha Stewart, Ray has the basic tenets of being a good host and girlfriend down pat.[1]

But Alessandra Stanley, the television critic for *The New York Times*, had slightly more mixed feelings about both the show and its host. Stanley wrote:

> Ms. Ray's first show was beyond bubbly. Watching it was like opening a shaken bottle of club soda and having it fizz all over the room.
>
> On a set meant to look like a cozy, slightly tacky New York apartment (she said she decorated it herself), Ms. Ray casts herself as America's big sister. . . . She seems more like the hyperactive little sister who is compelled always to outshine and outdo her older siblings. . . .
>
> Ms. Ray's appeal is not aspirational, it's reassuring: she is not more skilled or refined than her viewers, just speedier and a lot more confident. . . .
>
> The frantically busy new talk-show format gives Ms. Ray's outsize personality more room to crow and plenty of guests and strangers to eclipse. For her

legions of passionately devoted fans, there is even more of her to love. For the not-so-silent majority of people who find her unbearable, the cooking parts, at least, are mercifully brief.[2]

The odds of any new talk show surviving the brutal battle for television ratings are slim at best, no matter what the reviews may say. For every successful daytime talk-show host, for every Oprah or Dr. Phil, dozens of unsuccessful ones have fallen by the wayside. As David Hixson pointed out in his article on daytime talk shows in the *St. James Encyclopedia of Pop Culture*, people as diverse as onetime *Beverly Hills 90210* actress Gabrielle Carteris, *Partridge Family* child star Danny Bonaduce, ex-*Cosby Show* kid Tempestt Bledsoe, Mark L. Walberg, Rolanda Watts, Gordon Elliott, Gayle King, Charles Perez, Carnie Wilson of the pop group Wilson Phillips, former Pittsburgh Steelers quarterback Terry Bradshaw, Jim J. Bullock and Tammy Faye Baker Messner, George Hamilton and Alana Stewart, Vicki Lawrence, and Marsha Warfield have all tried and failed to find audiences for their own talk shows.

Despite these odds, when the ratings came out at the end of her first week on the air, it was apparent that *Rachael Ray* was going to be a major hit. Among all 13 talk shows then on the air, Ray's show finished fourth, behind only *The Oprah Winfrey Show*, *Dr. Phil*, and *Live with Regis & Kelly*. She had the highest-rated debut since Dr. Phil first went on the air in September 2002. It was clear that Ray's fans from the Food Network were eager to watch her as a talk-show host as well. Her numbers held and grew throughout the year, and when it came time to renew shows for the next season, hers was the only one of the four that debuted in 2006 to make it to the 2007 season. As she had done many times in her life, Rachael Ray had taken a chance against long odds and gone on to become an even bigger success.

On her talk show *Rachael Ray*, the host appears with First Lady Laura Bush during the first season. Over the years, many daytime talk shows have come and gone, but Ray's has been a success from the start. Of the four talk shows that debuted in the 2006–2007 season, only *Rachael Ray* was picked up for a second season.

OVERACHIEVER

Then again, Rachael Ray is nothing if not an overachiever. Since making her debut on the Food Network in November 2001 with *30-Minute Meals*, Ray has gone on to "star" in three other series for the network, *$40 a Day*, *Inside Dish*, and *Tasty Travels*, seen by an estimated 18 million viewers per week. She has written 15 best-selling cookbooks, introduced her own food and lifestyle magazine, *Every Day with Rachael Ray*, and endorsed everything from her own line of pots and pans and knives to Dunkin' Donuts and Burger

King, all in addition to hosting her own daily syndicated talk show. And she has accomplished all this before the age of 40 and without receiving any kind of formal chef's education.

While Ray has become one of America's most popular and influential chefs and television personalities in just a few short years, she is not without her critics. Many professional chefs dismiss Ray for her lack of formal training and for not taking cooking "seriously." Others mock her consistently "perky" personality and her ever-growing list of endorsements. Chef and television personality Anthony Bourdain, himself a graduate of the prestigious Culinary Institute of America, has referred to Ray as a "bobblehead" and attacked her endorsement of Dunkin' Donuts, telling *Outside* magazine that "she's got a magazine, a TV empire, all these best-selling books—I'm guessing she's not hurting for money. She's hugely influential, particularly with children. And she's endorsing Dunkin' Donuts. It's like endorsing crack for kids."[3]

Even her defenders, like Jill Hunter Pellettieri, writing for the online magazine *Slate*, feel obliged to address the criticisms of Ray, pointing out that "Rachael Ray may be the world's most reviled chef. . . . Professional chefs . . . turn up their noses when Ray comes around. It's easy to see why: Ray rejects specialty ingredients, elaborate recipes, and other foodie staples." "But," Pellettieri goes on to write, "she deserves our respect. She understands how Americans really cook, and she's an exceptional entertainer."[4]

Indeed, as Pellettieri points out:

Ray's marquee program, *30-Minute Meals*, relies on countless foodie no-nos. She advocates store-bought shortcuts—"I take a little help where I can get it"— using boxed corn muffin mix for her "Cracked Corn and Cheese Squares," and chunky peanut butter in her "Thai Salad with Peanut Dressing." She loathes baking—it's too fussy—so her "homemade" desserts are things like "Black Cherry Ice Cream with Chocolate Sauce": Buy the ice cream and top with chocolate sauce and a dash of cherry liqueur (ReddiWip is optional). Her dishes rely solely on items available at the local Safeway.[5]

But that, in a nutshell, is what makes Ray so popular. Armed with an almost alarmingly bubbly personality, she makes simple, tasty cooking accessible and available to people who might normally be intimidated by more so-called gourmet cooking. By taking the mystique and difficulty out of cooking and by using ingredients that are readily available in small-town America, she encourages people to cook new dishes, to try new recipes, to expand their normal dinner routine.

As superchef Mario Batali pointed out in his portrait of Ray for *Time* magazine's 2006 list of the "100 People Who Shape Our World":

In fewer than five years, Rachael Ray, 38, has radically changed the way America cooks dinner. Her perky-girl-next-door swagger, her catchphrases for techniques, and her dinner ideology of simpler, less expensive, and just in time have sold billions of books and placed her at the top of the talent love heap at the Food Network . . .

Ray dresses like a suburban American—not a chef (that is key)—and her ease with kitchen techniques and a simple-to-find-in-Topeka ingredient list does not challenge viewers but entices them to join her in the famous "carry the stuff from the fridge to the counter" move with her anti-food-stylist packaged groceries. The promise of a meal in less than 30 min.

Rachael Ray and chef Mario Batali attended a benefit for Ray's Yum-O! Organization in April 2008 at Barbuto, a restaurant in New York City. Although other chefs have criticized Ray for her lack of training, Batali has defended her. He says that Ray, with her 30-Minute Meals, has gotten more people into the kitchen and has changed the way people cook.

is delivered every day and is calculated to hit all those who ever had a family or thought of having one, coaxing them to eschew the trap of fast-food facility and truly cook—even the easy fast stuff—at home.[6]

Batali expanded on his praise of Ray in an interview with CNN personality Larry King, saying that "Rachael empowers people who don't want to watch my show and learn how

IRON CHEF AMERICA AND RACHAEL RAY

One of the most popular shows on the Food Network, *Iron Chef America: The Series*, is an American cooking competition based on Japanese television's *Iron Chef*, which appeared on the Food Network in a dubbed version.

Like the original Japanese show, the program is a sort of culinary game show/competition. In each episode, a new challenger chef "battles" one of the resident "Iron Chefs" in a one-hour cook-off, based around a theme ingredient: perhaps pork chops, or shrimp, or something as simple as an egg. Each chef is required to make a minimum of five dishes using the theme ingredient; then a panel of judges decides which chef wins, or "reigns supreme."

On November 12, 2006, the Food Network ran a special 90-minute episode of *Iron Chef America* that pitted two guest Food Network stars, Giada De Laurentiis and Rachael Ray, against each other, each of them teamed with one of the show's resident Iron Chefs. De Laurentiis, whose programs include *Everyday Italian*, *Behind the Bash*, and *Giada's Weekend Getaways*, was teamed with Bobby Flay; Ray with her old friend Mario Batali. Ray was terrified. The only untrained chef among the four participants, she was to cook; she teaches them how to cook. . . . Rachael takes things that you can find in every grocery store in America, makes them into an interesting food item and makes it, I believe, probably under the most important condition, time frame."[7]

David Carr of *The New York Times* elaborated on this idea of time in a 2006 article entitled "Rachael Ray Gives the Gift of Time":

certain that she was completely out of her element and was facing nothing but televised embarrassment and defeat.

The theme ingredient for the show was cranberries. Ray started out making a cranberry curd, which is a thickened custard to be used in a dessert. Much to her dismay, the curd did not thicken as quickly as she had hoped, leaving her far less time than she wanted to prepare her other two dishes: a cranberry pasta and shrimp served over cranberry polenta. (Polenta is an Italian dish of cornmeal mush.) Ray was certain that she and Batali would be going down in defeat and that the blame would rest entirely on her shoulders.

But to her great surprise, when the judging was finished and the votes were counted, she and Batali were the winners. Batali graciously gave the credit to Ray, saying that although her cranberry curd might have taken a while to make, in his opinion, the dish was the one that pushed them over the top to victory. Ray was completely shocked, relieved, and elated by the results. And while she says that she does not regret the experience, she admits that appearing on the program was the scariest thing she has ever done on the Food Network; she vows never to do it again.

Ms. Ray's folksy approach belies the sophistication of her message. She is part of the cut-to-the-chase genre of media . . . [which] is built on this fact of modern life: if people are more secure economically, it is only because they are working longer and harder than ever before. Lifestyle porn is fine and all—who wouldn't want to have that epic downtown loft in *Architectural Digest* or those lemon caper calamari steaks in *Gourmet*?—but even if you can afford the ingredients, you can't afford the time to conjure them before dinner.

Ms. Ray's recipes may call for store-bought turkey loaf, but she is really trafficking in the ultimate modern luxury: time. . . . The pitch for her show in [her] magazine pretty much sums the ethos up, suggesting viewers will "realize that life just doesn't have to be that hard." Of course, life is plenty hard, which is why a woman who tends to find succor in a slurp of store-bought pasta is hitting a sweet spot.[8]

Obviously, Rachael Ray represents many things to many people, and even more obviously, she has struck a chord within the American psyche. It is difficult to believe that just a little more than 10 years before being named by *Time* magazine as one of the 100 people who have shaped our world; just a little more than 10 years before the debut of her talk show lifted her from the ranks of television chef to media superstar, Rachael Ray was a college dropout working at the candy counter of Macy's in New York City, uncertain about what it was that she wanted to do with her life.

In retrospect, of course, her choice of career seems apparent—in fact, it seems just as likely that her career chose her. Ray grew up in restaurants, surrounded by great cooks, and cooking was always a natural and integral part of her life; her career, in a sense, was just a logical progression of her life. From cooking at home with her mom, to cooking demonstrations at local food markets, to cooking shows on television, Ray's life has revolved around food and encouraging others to cook and eat and love food just as much as she does.

But how did she do it? How did an untrained cook growing up in small towns in upstate New York go on to become one of the Food Network's biggest stars? How did she go from obscurity to being one of America's most liked as well as disliked media personalities? What is EVOO? What is stoup? Is "Yum-O" a good thing? And perhaps most intriguing, what role has she played in America's ongoing food revolution? Then again, what is a food revolution anyway?

A Food Revolution

Looking out over America's culinary landscape, it's difficult to believe just how much the country's eating habits have changed over the last 60 years.

Just think about it. Today, salsa is more popular than ketchup. Ethnic cuisines of all kinds—Italian, Chinese, Mexican, Indian, Thai, Vietnamese, and many others—have all become part of our everyday diets, at home and in restaurants. Grocery stores carry a wide range of ethnic cooking ingredients, and ingredients that were once considered exotic, like chipotle peppers and wasabi, have been incorporated into everyday items like mayonnaise. Sushi is sold in the take-out departments of most grocery stores. Fresh herbs, mushrooms, and a wider range of produce than ever before are now available to most shoppers. It is a whole new world.

Cooking and cuisine were very different just decades ago. Women did the cooking—it was close to unthinkable for an American man to know how to cook. Fast-food restaurants as we know them today did not exist. Ethnic cuisines were unknown outside of the largest cities. Spicy food was rarely eaten. And as hard as it might be to imagine, in an April 21, 1939, column in the *New York Herald Tribune*, food editor Clementine Paddleford felt it necessary to say that "if someone suggests a 'pizza pie' after the theatre, don't think it is going to be a wedge of apple. It is going to be the surprise of your life." She went on to explain that pizza would be "a nice stunt to surprise the visiting relatives, who will be heading East soon for the World's Fair. They come to be surprised, and pizza pronounced 'peet-za' will do the job up brown."[1]

As David Kamp points out in his book *The United States of Arugula: How We Became a Gourmet Nation*, the fact that Paddleford felt it necessary to explain how to pronounce pizza in a column aimed at supposedly educated diners says a lot about the American diet of the time. It was a world, as Kamp writes, where "dining out was for special occasions, ordering in was nearly unheard of, and most Americans adhered to a diet of what was familiar to them locally and culturally. Italian foods such as 'peet-za' were alien to all but Italian Americans and a small minority of urban culinary adventurers. To America's wealthy elite, eating Italian food was beneath contempt, irredeemably déclassé and stinky."[2]

For most Americans, a good meal consisted of a simply prepared dish of meat and potatoes. Food was not something to be enjoyed: Eating was done in order to fuel the body. Then, as the 1940s, 1950s, and 1960s progressed, busy housewives began to turn away from fresh foods and produce and to rely increasingly on the convenience of newly introduced canned and frozen foods and dinners.

(Sales of fresh fruit, for example, dropped from 140 pounds, or 63.5 kilograms, per person per year in the 1940s to just 90 pounds, or 41 kilograms, in the 1960s. The difference was made up in sales of canned fruits, often sold in heavy, sugary syrup.) It became unfashionable to spend time in the kitchen making a home-cooked meal, as busy housewives, with the help of persuasive advertising, came more and more to rely on easy-to-prepare convenience foods to get dinner on the table.

At the same time, though, in places like New York City and among the elite of those cities, interest in "gourmet" food was growing. The end of World War II saw an influx of chefs from Europe, as well as of soldiers returning home who had eaten and enjoyed the still "exotic" foods of Europe. French restaurants of a quality never before seen in the United States began to open in New York City, and a clientele eager to publicly display their sophistication flocked to them. A divide began to open up between a cultural elite becoming more food-aware and the majority of Americans, living largely on simple "American" food, processed foods, and take-out foods from rapidly expanding restaurants like McDonald's and Kentucky Fried Chicken.

It was the late 1950s that saw the early beginnings of the food revolution, of food suddenly becoming "trendy." Writer Nora Ephron brilliantly described the process in her 1968 essay "The Food Establishment":

In the 1950s, suddenly, no one knew quite why or how, everyone began to serve curry. Dinner parties in fashionable homes featured curried lobster. Dinner parties in middle-income homes featured curried chicken. Dinner parties in frozen-food compartments featured curried rice. And with the arrival of curry, the first fashionable international food, food acquired a chic, a gloss of snobbery it had hitherto possessed only in certain upper-income groups.[3]

But while curry was all well and good, French food was still the benchmark of what was considered fine cuisine, and it was thought to be out of the reach of the average home chef. Beginning in 1963, however, a tall, ungainly woman appeared on public television, and she would change the way Americans cooked, by demonstrating that they, too, could cook gourmet French food at home.

THE FRENCH CHEF

Her name was Julia Child. Six-foot-four, with a cheery manner and a distinctively high-pitched, warbly voice, she seemed an unlikely person to influence America's eating habits. Born in 1912 in Pasadena, California, she grew up eating traditional New England food prepared by the family maid. After marrying Paul Cushing Child, she moved with him in 1948 to France, where he was assigned to work by the U.S. State Department.

It was in the city of Rouen that she had a meal—oysters, sole meunière (a delicate fish with a sauce of butter and lemon), salad, and cheese—that profoundly changed her way of thinking about food. "I couldn't get over it," Child recalled years later. It was, as she told *The New York Times*, "an opening up of the soul and spirit for me."[4] In Paris, she attended the famous Le Cordon Bleu cooking school and studied privately with master chefs. She joined the women's cooking club *Cercle des Gourmettes*, where she met Simone Beck, who, along with her friend Louisette Bertholle, was writing a French cookbook for Americans: the two Frenchwomen proposed that Child work with them to help make it American-friendly.

In 1951, the trio began to teach cooking to American women in the Childs' Paris kitchen, all the while researching

Cooking personality Julia Child prepared a French delicacy during a November 1970 taping of her program, *The French Chef*, one of the first cooking shows on television. With her TV shows and books, Child had a tremendous influence on the eating and cooking habits of Americans.

and testing recipes that Child translated from French into English, working to make the recipes detailed, interesting, and above all, practical. Their work took them the better part of a decade.

The three authors initially signed a contract with Houghton Mifflin, which later rejected the 800-page manuscript as too big and expensive to publish; the company could not imagine that there was an American market for such a book. Child sent the manuscript to the publishing house Alfred A. Knopf, where it turned up on the desk of editor Judith Jones, who had long been looking for such a book. "When I came back from living in France," said Jones, quoted in *The United States of Arugula*, "I realized that there wasn't really a book that taught you how to cook French food at home. So I got this in 1960 and thought, 'This is it!'"[5]

The book, titled *Mastering the Art of French Cooking*, was published in 1961, becoming a surprise best seller and a tremendous critical success. Praised for its helpful illustrations, its precise attention to detail, and its ability to make fine cooking available to the masses, the book profited in no small part from a growing interest in French culture and food in the early 1960s. Indeed, first lady Jacqueline Kennedy had made headlines that same year by hiring a Frenchman, René Verdon, to be the official White House chef. (Verdon himself was surprised by the sudden growth of interest in French food, noting that "when I came to America in 1958, people were talking more about gravy than sauces, but that changed fast."[6])

Based on the book's success, Child began to write magazine articles and a regular column for *The Boston Globe* newspaper. But it was a 1962 appearance on a book-review show on the Public Broadcasting Service (PBS) station of Boston, WGBH, that led to the inception of the television cooking show that made her a star.

The show, called *The French Chef*, was one of the first cooking shows on television. Through television, Child made the art of French cooking accessible to a wide range of viewers. Her audience, eager to practice what they learned, stormed cookware stores, demanding the equipment that Child had used on that week's show. Likewise, grocers were faced with requests for shallots, fresh herbs, and whatever ingredients Child's recipes required. The food revolution, which had fitfully begun in the late 1950s, was now in full bloom. As Nora Ephron said in *The United States of Arugula*, "Curry opened the door for this gourmet transformation.

In the late fifties and early sixties, sophisticated cooking became *the* thing to do: you were an adult, and therefore you cooked."[7]

NEW CUISINES, NEW TASTES

As America's palate became more sophisticated, new flavors, cuisines, and ingredients became part of the food scene. The appreciation of Italian food, once confined to inexpensive restaurants serving spaghetti and pizza, became more sophisticated as Americans discovered its full range and variety. Chinese food went beyond chow mein and egg rolls as the spicy, flavorful foods of Hunan and Szechwan were embraced by intrepid foodies. Mexican, Thai, Japanese—all became part of mainstream dining.

Along with the new cuisines came new ingredients. Items like balsamic vinegar, sun-dried tomatoes, hoisin sauce, arugula, kiwis, brie, chutneys, and prosciutto went from being exotic ingredients to everyday items found in most major grocery stores. Salads went from wedges of iceberg lettuce floating in Thousand Island dressing to carefully composed mixtures of baby greens. Tuna noodle casserole was replaced by grilled tuna cooked rare, or even eaten raw, as in Japanese sushi.

New concepts sprang up as well. From Alice Waters in Berkeley, California, came the idea of sustainable food. Instead of purchasing food from farmers across the country, produce designed to ship well but with little flavor, Waters preached the gospel of eating only seasonal, locally grown ingredients, served in the freshest state possible. Organic food grew in popularity as well, as more and more people grew alarmed at the additives and chemicals in so much of our food. The idea of eating well, of good food as part of the good life, has become essential in many of our lives.

Another factor in America's food revolution is how rapidly culinary trends and ingredients spread, moving from gourmet stores and upper-end restaurants to chain restaurants and regular supermarkets. As *New York Times* restaurant critic Frank Bruni pointed out in his review of Food Network star Bobby Flay's restaurant Mesa Grill, "Its Southwestern swirl of peppery rubs and smoky glazes, of tropical sweetness and desert fire, have been popularized to the point of cliché. It informed the menu of Chi-Chi's, Chili's, and Chipotle."[8] Indeed, when an ingredient such as the chipotle chile, unknown to most Americans just a few years ago, is offered by McDonald's in its Chipotle BBQ Snack Wrap, it is apparent just how quickly new food items are entering the culinary mainstream.

But this is not to say that the food revolution has touched all Americans. As David Kamp observes in *The United States of Arugula*, eating in America is moving along two very different tracks. Many Americans subsist largely on junk food and fast food, getting fatter and fatter as they try one diet after another, eating too many processed foods, and lacking the knowledge, the time, and the self-confidence in the kitchen to take advantage of the wonderful array of products now available to cook interesting, healthy meals.

IN HER OWN WORDS

Rachael Ray, with her she's-just-like-you appeal, is bringing the food revolution to a whole new group of people. As she said in an interview with *The Seattle Times*:

> People don't look at me and think, "That's so fancy" and "I could never do that." They think, "I could totally do that."

A display of exotic and organic fruit is a highlight of the produce section at this Hannaford supermarket in Concord, New Hampshire. As people's tastes have become more sophisticated, more and more new ingredients and products are available in the supermarket down the street.

On the other track, of course, are the so-called foodies, who have gourmet kitchens loaded with the latest equipment, subscribe to all the food magazines, watch cooking shows on television, keep abreast of all the newest culinary trends, and do not hesitate to spend hours in the kitchen making the perfect meal. They may be a minority, but they are a very visible minority, and their lifestyle is one that many aspire to.

But is there a middle ground between the two groups? Frankly, most people have neither the time nor the money necessary to prepare gourmet food on a nightly basis, yet they are dissatisfied with a diet of take-out and processed foods. Like a hungry man with his nose pressed against the window of a restaurant watching patrons eating plates of delicious food, they too would like to become a part of America's food revolution. It would be Rachael Ray's role to help spread the food revolution beyond the ranks of the confirmed foodies.

Growing Up
with Food

Rachael Ray, born Rachael Domenica Ray on August 25, 1968, on Cape Cod, Massachusetts, was born lucky. Unlike many of her generation who grew up eating fast food, packaged food, and junk food, she grew up surrounded by people who loved to cook and loved to eat. If the saying "born in a trunk" is applied to the children of actors who are destined to follow in their parents' theatrical footsteps, "born in a kitchen" definitely applies to Rachael.

Her mother was the oldest of 10 children whose father, Emmanuel, was an immigrant who had worked as a stonemason in his native Sicily. Rachael's father, James Ray, of Welsh, Scottish and French/Cajun background, grew up in Louisiana. The three main adults in Rachael's life would have a profound impact on her love of food.

The head of a family of 12, Rachael's grandfather was the main chef of the family. He grew his own vegetables and taught Rachael's mom how to cook. "My mom was the eldest of 10, and my grandfather taught her because she was the first," Ray said in an interview with Larry King. "You know she was always in the kitchen with him, and he was phenomenal."[1]

In an interview with Beverly Keel for *American Profile*, Ray elaborated on her grandfather's culinary influence. "My cooking comes from my grandfather and my mom. They were both amazing cooks. I don't know if she could do everything in 30 minutes or not, but she is definitely great, and she knows every dish. There is nothing she can't make."[2]

The influence that Rachael's grandfather had on her went far beyond food. Her entire family attests to the fact that she is like him in many ways, especially in their smiles, their laugh, and their sheer gusto for life. In a television biography aired on the Food Network, Rachael discussed her grandfather's great laugh, and said that, when she was a very little girl, he would have no tolerance for any of her "drama." If she was crying, he would just laugh, and if she was pouting, he would tickle her.

Rachael's taste buds and love of cooking were not just influenced by the Italian cuisine of her grandfather and mother. From growing up in Louisiana, Rachael's father had absorbed all of the culinary strands that make up Louisiana cooking: spicy Cajun food, sophisticated Creole food, and the down-home goodness of Southern cooking. As Ray said in an interview with Knight Ridder Newspapers, "All of us have big tempers and love spicy food."[3] Along with her older sister, Maria (eight years her senior), and her younger brother, Emmanuel (six years younger), Rachael grew up surrounded by food and cooking. When she was

Rachael Ray's smile is almost as famous as her 30-Minute Meals. That smile, her family says, is one she shared with her grandfather. They also shared the same enjoyment of life and the same love of food. Here, Ray rode a Zamboni machine in January 2008 during the taping of her special, *Rachael Ray on Ice.*

a young girl, the family owned a chain of three restaurants on Cape Cod called The Carvery, and both parents worked in them, bringing the family with them as often as possible. Not surprisingly, one of Rachael's first memories involves cooking and food, and what was probably her first accident in the kitchen, as she revealed in an interview with *Good Housekeeping* magazine:

> My mom used to do this neat thing where she would take a piece of provolone or Swiss cheese, fry it up, then pinch it in the middle. We'd call them cheese

bow ties. I loved them. But one day, when I was a toddler, I was in a restaurant kitchen with her, and I saw a spatula. I thought, Oh, there's that thing Mom uses to make cheese bow ties, and I started to mimic her. Next thing you know, I had grilled my own thumb on the griddle.[4]

Not only that, but Rachael's first word was "vino!"—the Italian word for wine.

She was known for her giggly, happy little face, and hanging out in her parents' restaurants gave her ample opportunity to get into mischief. One family story is about a favorite prank of Rachael's when she was little. One restaurant had a big picture window with curtains. Rachael would hide behind the curtain and wait for people to sit at the table by the window. As soon as they did, she would rip the curtain open and greet them with a cheery "Hello, buckaroos!"

Growing up eating great Italian and Louisiana food caused occasional difficulties when Rachael went to school. Rachael was considered a good student and a talented creative artist (she was also rather mature for her age, when she wasn't being too bossy). Still, lunchtime caused a few problems. "I wouldn't eat junk," Rachael told *Good Housekeeping*. "In fact, when I first went to school, I came home upset because the food was terrible. I'd never seen white bread before."[5] But not only was she upset by the usual school cafeteria fare, her schoolmates were equally upset when they saw what she was bringing in her lunchbox, as she told *People* magazine:

I had the lunchbox that cleared the cafeteria. I was very unpopular in the early grades. . . . Because I hung out with my grandfather, I started to bring my lunchbox with sardine sandwiches and calamari that I would eat off my fingers like rings. I was also always reeking of garlic. I sat alone but that's okay, I sat alone with good food![6]

Rachael had other reasons for being alone as well. Throughout her early childhood, she often suffered from croup, a respiratory disease that left a permanent mark on Ray: her distinctive husky voice. Croup is treated by inhaling hot steam, so her parents would construct a vaporizing tent, made of a broomstick and sheets, on her bed. There she would sit by herself and think and draw. She was, as her mother said in *Vanity Fair* magazine, always "drawing something or writing something. She was always doing that."[7]

Not only was she always drawing or writing, she was also always observant, always watching what was going on around her. When she was five or six, her mother gave her a book called *The Casual Observer*. It told the story of a little girl who traveled the world, observing and meeting people and always asking questions along the way. Rachael described the book's influence in an interview with *Budget Travel*:

One day when I went to school, my teachers asked me to draw a picture of what I wanted to be when I grew up, so I drew a picture of this weird little girl with a bonnet on. My teacher said, "So what do you want to be?" And I said, "A casual observer!" I always thought that it was a real profession, but I think I became very much what I wanted to be.[8]

Despite her childhood illnesses, Rachael was by all accounts an extraordinarily happy child. "The minute she was up she wanted to be where you were," her mother, Elsa Scuderi, told *Vanity Fair*. "And whatever was happening she wanted to be around that."[9] And while the family never had a lot of money, Rachael has always felt that her childhood was rich and happy. Once a year, her mom would take her to New York City, where she would get to see a Broadway show and then pick out one item from the legendary toy store FAO Schwarz. From this, Rachael learned what is, for her, the secret of having a happy life even if you're not wealthy.

"You can have a wonderful, much better quality of life than you think," Ray told *The Seattle Times*. "You really do think you lead a rich life if you do something as simple as making dinner for yourself. You don't have to be left out of anything. Maybe you can't stay in a five-star suite, maybe you can just sit in the cocktail lounge and look at the beautiful view, but you can still go there."[10] This attitude of how to live has carried through her cookbooks, her travel shows, and her talk show.

Her once-a-year trips to New York City left one other impression as well: They left her with the desire to make her way one day to the big city. In a documentary about her life on the Biography Channel, she said that she was convinced that she would go there and something magical would happen to her. Little did she know that her dream would eventually come true, but not without a struggle.

SMALL-TOWN LIFE

By the mid-1970s, when Rachael was in second grade, the family had moved to Lake Luzerne, a small town (population 3,219 at the time of the 2000 census) in upstate New York, about 200 miles (322 kilometers) north of Manhattan. There, James Ray became the marketing director for a publisher. Rachael's mother, Elsa, stayed in the restaurant business, becoming the food supervisor for a group of restaurants owned by Carl DeSantis, a well-known entrepreneur and philanthropist. She remained in that position for more than 30 years: opening restaurants, planning their menus, and training their staffs.

Rachael's parents divorced when she was 13. "For a lot of people, divorce is traumatic," Ray told *Good Housekeeping*. "But for us, it made for a happier family. It was miserable to watch people live together who shouldn't."[11] The divorce was amicable, and Rachael's mom encouraged her to maintain her relationship with her father. Rachael says that she inherited her storytelling abilities from her dad. But from the man who could take six hours to grocery-shop and three days to make gumbo, there's one trait that the "queen of 30-Minute Meals" did *not* inherit from her father—a sense of patience.

As a working mom at a time when most women were stay-at-home mothers, Scuderi was reluctant to leave her children with a babysitter while she was busy running restaurants. Her solution? Take her children to work with her. "My mom took us to work with her because she didn't like to leave us with strangers,"[12] Ray explained to *Good Housekeeping*. So growing up, Rachael was often asked to fill in for dishwashers and waitresses on nights her mother was short-staffed.

She also learned how to cook. Indeed, given the importance that the family placed on good food, it's not surprising that all of the Ray siblings grew up cooking, although each has different strengths and weaknesses. (As Ray said in an article in *Newsweek*, "Food was always a conduit in our family for storytelling, and it was a way for us to keep in touch and remember things. We're people that use food to keep each other together and to always cheer us up and make all of our days better."[13]) Today, it is older sister Maria who is best at baking, which Rachael claims she stinks at, saying, "It's like the only thing that has ever made me cry besides pain or hardship."[14] Emmanuel specializes in slow-cooking, and Rachael boasts that she can take any recipe and "canoodle it" (meaning that she can simplify a recipe and make it faster to prepare, so it is accessible for the average American cook).

Cooking with her mom is the only culinary training that Rachael ever had. In an interview with Lisa McKinnon of the *Ventura County Star*, Ray called her mother "the head chef of the only cooking school I've ever attended."[15] Rachael is confident that that was all the training she ever needed. "I learned everything about cooking basically at home and in restaurants," she said in an interview for *American Profile*. "A lot of people ask me where I learned how to cook. My mother never showed me how to peel a potato. There was never, 'Try this, you'll like it.' There was just dinner: 'Here's what you're eating.' You didn't have to ask how to make it if you were in the kitchen, and everybody lived in the kitchen."[16]

By an early age, by example and by practice, Rachael was cooking on her own. She told *Good Housekeeping* about the first meal she ever made:

> I made my mom dinner when I was 12: lasagna roll-ups with a Gorgonzola sauce. I also made asparagus, and I remember fanning the spears out perfectly all around the plate. Today, I would never fuss with arranging asparagus, but I guess I had more patience at 12 than I do at 38.[17]

Making stuffed pasta filled with spinach and artichokes topped with a Gorgonzola sauce (a rich Italian blue cheese) is not a typical first meal for any beginning chef. Given the example that her mother set, though, it is not surprising that Rachael set her sights high.

Her mother was, and still is, Rachael's role model. "I wanted to be just like my mother," she said in an interview with *Reader's Digest*. "She was loud and fierce, a great piece of work. She was four-foot-eleven in stiletto heels, which she always wore, and she did the work of any 12 men."[18]

Indeed, as much as she learned about cooking from her mom, she learned something equally valuable. She learned from her mother an ethos of hard work. As Laura Jacobs pointed out in her profile of Ray for *Vanity Fair*, "Regarding Rachael there are two recurring themes in the Ray family. 'Day one,' says her older sister, Maria Betar, 'we knew that she was just going somewhere and doing something. She's always risen to the top.' Theme two: 'She tends to be almost passionate to a fault,' says younger brother Manny Ray. Her father elaborates: 'She's the hardest-working person I know.' "[19]

THE CULINARY INSTITUTE OF AMERICA

Rachael Ray has found tremendous success as a chef without the benefit of formal culinary training. For most aspiring chefs, though, going to culinary school is the surest path to a successful career. To many, the Culinary Institute of America (known as the CIA) is considered one of the finest places in the United States at which to receive a top-notch culinary education.

Founded in 1946 in Hyde Park, New York, with satellite campuses in St. Helena, California, San Antonio, Texas, and New York City, the CIA offers classes taught by the world's largest staff of American Culinary Federation Certified Master Chefs. The college offers Bachelor of Professional Studies (B.P.S.) and Associate of Occupational Studies (A.O.S.) degrees in either culinary arts or baking and pastry arts. Admission to the school requires a minimum of six months' food-service experience. In addition, the program also requires an 18-week externship at a CIA-approved facility in the food industry.

Learning occurs in other places besides the classroom. The CIA operates five restaurants that are open to the public at its

That is something she learned by example from her mother. "She always worked 100 hours a week, even though she was paid for 40. She did it because there was still work to be done," Ray told *Good Housekeeping*. And the same applies to Ray today. "It doesn't matter what job I have. I enjoy work. I like going to bed really tired."[20]

Even while growing up, she was on the lookout for opportunities to make it big. When she was in her teens, she wrote a letter to John Peterman, simply because she was a fan of the J. Peterman clothing catalog. The title of her

campus in Hyde Park. There, students gain experience in back-of-the-house kitchen work and front-of-the-house management skills. The restaurants offer students the opportunity to cook in a wide range of cuisines, including American, French, and Italian. Through working in real restaurants, the students are able to apply the skills they have learned in their classes, giving them a complete education and adding to their ability to find work in the highly competitive world of restaurants. Indeed, among the graduates of the Culinary Institute of America are many of the most respected and well-known chefs, including Anthony Bourdain, Michael Chiarello, Cat Cora, Rocco DiSpirito, Todd English, Sara Moulton, and Michael Symon.

The CIA offers more than just professional education for aspiring restaurant chefs. The school also offers recreational classes for the non-professional home chef. The institute sells books, videos, and training manuals created by the faculty and staff, allowing access to the kind of education that can make anybody a better cook.

Students in traditional white chef's garb work at a table laden with food at the Culinary Institute of America in Hyde Park, New York. Besides taking coursework, students at the institute have the opportunity to get real-life experience by working in one of five restaurants.

letter? "Little Girl, Big Ideas." Just a few years later, she took a chance and wrote a letter to Harry Connick Sr., who was then the New Orleans district attorney. Rachael had dreams of opening a jazz supper club in nearby Saratoga Springs, and she asked Connick to send his son, jazz musician Harry Connick Jr., to perform. It is clear that Rachael was always someone who, when she knew what she wanted, was not afraid to take a chance on going out and getting it.

Not only does her love of hard work trace back to her childhood, so also does her impatience, her desire to do as much as possible, all of which led to her goal of getting dinner on the table in just 30 minutes. While growing up, for example, Rachael, like many young girls, took dance class. She complained, though, about how long lessons took, saying that "I don't want to do any more exercises. I want to dance."[21]

Along with dance, she wanted to cook. She loved to bake chocolate chip cookies with her younger brother, Manny, even though there was never that much actual baking involved. The problem would be that the two of them loved eating the raw cookie dough so much, they were lucky if as many as six cookies made it to the oven.

Rachael was close to her older sister as well. One of her favorite memories is of her sitting in the passenger seat while her sister drove an old car with a stick shift. The two would stop at a local bakery, purchase a cheap "damaged" birthday cake, and spend the rest of the day driving around, listening to music and taking turns shifting while they ate the entire cake directly out of the box with their hands. And this was a cake that was meant to be eaten by 14 people.

Rachael did have other interests besides food. Not surprisingly, given her go-getting, cheerfully energetic television image, Rachael was a cheerleader in high school, just as her mother had been. It seems that, in all things, Rachael wanted to be just like her mother. For Rachael, her mom was not just her mom. She was (and is) her role model, her teacher, her best friend. Rachael paid tribute to Elsa on her Food Network biography, stating that her mother taught her how to be adventurous, how to travel well, how not to be afraid of going out in the world, and how to take a little and make it into a lot. She said:

Everything that I do and say in my life today, how I make my living, how I live my personal life, it was all influenced by my Mom. If she had been born just a few years later, all this work would actually be her life. She's really the original. She's a better cook than I am, she's a better decorator than I am. I think she'd be a more successful Rachael Ray than I am.[22]

Surrounded by a loving family, hardworking and actively involved in school activities, Rachael led a surprisingly normal life, with just one small exception. For most teenagers, getting their first driver's license is an important milestone—one more step on the road to independence. When Rachael went to take her road test, however, she accidentally ran over a cat, killing it. She was so upset and felt so bad that she simply abandoned the car in the middle of the street, refusing to finish. Rachael did not pass her test and was so traumatized by the event that she did not go back to retake her exam.

Upon graduating from Lake George High School in 1986, and being voted "most artistic" by her classmates, Rachael had some important decisions to make. Now that high school was over, what was she going to do with her life?

GETTING OUT

At this stage of life, like most young people, Rachael was unsure what direction her life was going to take. She knew she wanted a career, even though she was not certain that it meant becoming a chef. From the outside, being a restaurant chef can appear to be a glamorous position. But seen from the inside, as Rachael had her entire life, she knew that being a chef in a restaurant is a job that demands long hours of work over a hot stove. Was that what she wanted for herself?

On the other hand, there was one thing that Rachael *was* certain about. Although she knew she wanted to continue her education, she was not yet ready to move too far from home. She would have to find a way to continue her education while still maintaining her small-town life. Living in an upstate New York town, though, she knew her options were limited.

Life in the Big City

Rachael Ray settled on Pace University, a small, coeducational university in the New York metropolitan area with campuses in New York City and Westchester County, New York. Pace is best known for its programs in environmental law, nursing, and business, and it is the home of the Actors Studio MFA program and the television show *Inside the Actors Studio*. Ray spent the next couple of years taking classes in literature and communications at Pace's Westchester County campus, while still working nearly full time. She ran and operated her own company named "Delicious Liaisons," which offered gift baskets of pasta and cocoa mix accompanied by her own hand-lettered catalogs, while also working in a variety of restaurant jobs—even bartending on a lake boat. But she soon realized that college was not for her.

Pace was not inexpensive, and since Ray was still plagued by doubts as to her future, "it was more like I was going to school for hobbies," she told *Vanity Fair*. "I didn't know what I wanted to do."[1] And since thriftiness has always been a part of her personality, she decided it was time to leave school after two years, move to New York City, get a job, and try to save her money until she knew exactly what she wanted to do.

It was time for her to be out on her own. Living in a small upstate New York town, well aware of the limits of small-town life, and faced with the possibility of getting trapped in a series of low-paying jobs, Ray was eager to get out and make a fresh start. She knew that it was time for her to be on her own, to test herself by living away from her family, and she was ready to explore all the possibilities and excitement that living in New York City had to offer.

Thanks to her years of experience working with her mother ("I was surrounded by all different styles of cooking and worked in the food service industry in just about every capacity you can imagine," she says on her magazine's Web site[2]), Ray had no trouble finding work. Managing a bar, waitressing at Howard Johnson's—she did it all. None of these jobs were entirely satisfying, though, and none of them provided her with a clear indication of which direction her life would go. That would come in the early 1990s, when she saw a small ad in *The New York Times* for a job that would be the first real step in her career.

BEHIND THE COUNTER

One of the results of America's ongoing food revolution was the need for new stores and outlets—new high-end "gourmet" food markets to meet the demands of shoppers for high-quality, occasionally "exotic" ingredients. One of the nation's oldest and most well-known department stores, Macy's, quickly jumped on the bandwagon.

From its humble beginnings as a dry goods store in Haverhill, Massachusetts, in 1851, Macy's had quickly expanded, until, with the completion of an addition to its flagship store in Herald Square, New York City, in 1924, it was able to bill itself as the "world's largest store" with one million square feet of selling space. By constantly evolving to meet new consumer demands, the store, now a nation-wide chain, was able to maintain its position of leadership among American department stores.

As America's culinary interests expanded throughout the 1960s and '70s, Macy's saw the need to capitalize on a grow-ing market. Thus, in October 1976, Macy's Marketplace was born at the Herald Square store. Selling gourmet cookware, cheese and appetizers, delicatessen meats, sau-sages and pâtés, coffees and teas, high-end baked goods and candies, Macy's remodeled 10,000 square feet of space into a modern marketplace of tile, glass, and natural wood, devoted to the display and selling of fine foods.

"Food is part of a fashion image these days, and the really with-it person has to be interested," Edward Finkelstein, president of Macy's New York, said in 1976.[3] Indeed, the opening of Macy's Marketplace was such a major event that *The New York Times* sent its restaurant critic, Mimi Sheraton, to write a review of the trendsetting space. Sheraton raved about the market, having this to say about the candy counter in particular:

> Candy lovers are really in luck not only with the world's finest commercial chocolate, Lindt's, on hand in both bars and bonbons, but also in the array of candied fruits: whole pineapples and melons, green sticks of angelica, red cherries, golden cuts of citron, orange clementines.[4]

It was at Macy's candy counter that Rachael Ray got her start. (And it's interesting to note, just as an example of how quickly the desire for high-quality ingredients has spread throughout the country that Lindt's, once available only in high-end specialty markets such as Macy's, is now available in most supermarkets.)

"I saw this little ad in *The New York Times* for a candy-counter manager at Macy's," Ray told *Vanity Fair*, "and I thought, Well, I could do that."[5] She was just 23 years old when she interviewed for the job, and she vividly remembered the experience in *Chefography*, a biography program on the Food Network:

> It was like for $24,000 and I thought that was $9 million; to me that was just all the money in the world. So I went for the job interview and I remember my boss, Michael Corsello, interviewing me and asking me, "What makes you think that Mom and Pop store experience will make you ready for working at Macy's in our Marketplace?"
>
> "Well, (she replied), because I have a real eye and I always help my mother with buffets, and again, I know customers. I was a fantastic waitress and a very good hostess. I know how to deal with customers, and we have a retail section too, you know!" I got sort of combative with him—I think he thought I was funny.[6]

Corsello thought she was more than funny. He fell in love with her personality and decided to hire her on the spot.

Although she got the job, she did not hold onto it for long. The manager of the fresh foods department left, and Corsello was so impressed with Ray's work at the candy counter that he named her as a temporary replacement.

In 1991, Rachael Ray got a job working at the candy counter at Macy's Marketplace in the department store's flagship Herald Square location in Manhattan. Soon, she was promoted to run the fresh foods department. Ray enjoyed the work so much that she realized she wanted to pursue a career in the food business.

The job was a giant leap forward for Ray, with a great deal more responsibility, responsibility she may not have been ready for. As Ray said in her biography on the Food Network, "I ended up with a job that I didn't deserve. Michael told me that this is a job that you didn't deserve: just write the schedules, make sure they are posted, and that's it. Don't touch anything, don't do anything, don't think too much."[7]

Given Ray's personality and love of food, it seems unlikely that there was ever any chance that she would listen to his orders. No stranger to hard work, she worked harder than she ever had in her life, learning how to run the entire department and becoming conversant about upper-end food products like cheeses, smoked salmon, and caviar, all items that she was unfamiliar with. Learning everything, as *The New York Times* said, "from buying cheese to how to shop for Liza Minnelli's holiday food gifts,"[8] was the best crash course possible in high-end gourmet food. Ray was such a good student and quick learner that she got to keep the job.

Not only did she get to keep the job, she discovered herself in the process. After just a few weeks, she was on the phone with Elsa, telling her how well she was doing, how much she loved the job, how much she liked food, how much she liked working with food. At last, Ray knew what she wanted to do with her life. Food had long been her passion—now it would be her career.

Somewhat shockingly, though, almost as quickly as she found her career, she nearly lost it. Macy's was so impressed with Ray's work that store officials proposed giving her a promotion—right out of fresh foods and into women's clothing. The plan was to make her an accessories (purses, belts, hat, jewelry, etc.) buyer. Ray's response? "What did I know about that junk?" she said on *Chefography*.[9] Unwilling to move from food to women's clothing, she decided it was time to look for a new job.

At the same time, Corsello, the man who had hired her at Macy's, had since left to work in Washington, D.C. He tried to get Ray to follow him to D.C. to take a similar position there. Ray was so grateful to Corsello for giving her her start that she actually went to Washington to find about the new position. The job itself was great, and it paid about $60,000 a year, which would have been a huge raise in salary. The problem, though, was that the job required that she drive. Since she still felt extremely uncomfortable driving, and in fact did not have her license, she had to turn the position down, telling Corsello that "I can never take this job. It's the greatest job in the world, but I'll die. I won't survive a month here."[10]

CHANGES

Returning home to New York, Ray had an interview with Joe Musco, whose family, including his wife, Agata, and his daughter, Valentina, were planning to open a new gourmet store on New York City's fashionably expensive Upper East Side. The interview lasted for nearly nine hours as Ray and the entire Musco family bonded over their shared Sicilian heritage and mutual love of food. To no one's surprise, by the end of the interview, Ray had gotten the job.

She loved working at the store, called Agata & Valentina. She loved the Musco family. She loved the shop itself, with its atmosphere of a little Sicilian village and its wide range of products from Italy and around the world. Customers

IN HER OWN WORDS

Rachael Ray realized the direction she wanted her career to take while working in upscale establishments like Macy's Marketplace and Agata & Valentina. Yet she knows the appeal of comfort food. The Web site Pop Crazy asked Ray what her favorite dish to bring to a potluck dinner was. Her reply:

> Italian Mac-n-cheese—four cheeses, sausage, tomatoes, yum-o. It makes grown men cry.

flocked to the store, eager to purchase its wide range of Italian meats and cheeses, fresh homemade pastas, groceries and frozen foods—everything aspiring chefs and lovers of gourmet food needed to prepare and eat the finest Italian food. And Ray could do it all: She could buy anything, fix anything, get along with and earn the respect of all of her co-workers. Her career was going extraordinarily well—until an unfortunate series of events forced Ray to reconsider life in New York City.

One night, coming home late from work to her apartment in the New York City borough of Queens, Ray was confronted by a pair of teenage boys no older than 16 in the building's entryway. While Ray was looking for keys in her purse, one of the boys stuck a gun into her back and told her to give him all her money. Attached to her keys was a vial of pepper spray, so Ray began wildly spraying the pair of would-be robbers while screaming so loudly that, as she told *Vanity Fair*, "I scared myself."[11] The teenagers ran away, and Ray, shaken but unhurt, decided just to put the whole ugly incident behind her.

Ray's bad luck continued just three days after the mugging, when she broke her ankle falling off a chair, forcing her to move around on crutches. Then, less than two weeks after the initial robbery attempt, one of the muggers returned, but this time, Ray did not get away unscathed. The robber managed to drag Ray into a passage outside the building, where he hit her over and over with his pistol, all the while threatening to kill her. Once again, Ray screamed, and this time Lisa, the building's guard dog, responded: The dog's barking scared away the teenage robber, and Ray was forced to go to the hospital to have her injuries treated. With this second mugging in less than two weeks, Ray was unable to shake off the episode.

"Nothing so much happened," Ray told *Vanity Fair*. "People have a lot worse things in life. But it was like,

O.K., I'm not going to wait for strike three. I felt the whole universe was telling me, You're not supposed to be here right now."[12] It was a difficult time for Ray, who had been certain that life was going her way. She told *Chefography*, "I was on top of the world . . . got mugged twice, and said, eh . . . not quite so much on the top of the world anymore. Maybe New York's not for me."[13] Unable and unwilling to return to the scene of the crime, she had her family move her belongings out of her apartment. She never went back.

New York City, the city that had once seemed so promising, the city of such possibilities, the city that had given her a career, now seemed a dark and dangerous place. Ray was convinced that she would never return to New York. She would go back to her small-town roots, return home, and see what would happen there. She was warned that she would never be able to make it in business while living in upstate New York, but Ray was confident that she would succeed no matter where she lived. Little did she know, though, that moving back to upstate New York would turn out to be the first step toward stardom.

Birth of the
30-Minute Meal

Returning to the security of mom, family and home, Rachael Ray immediately began to rebuild her life in the only way she knew—by going back to work. She took whatever food-related jobs she could find: working in local restaurants, bartending, and managing Mister Brown's Pub in the historic landmark Sagamore Hotel, located on Lake George in the Adirondack Mountains. It was there, surrounded by the beauty of the mountains, that she was able to recover from the trauma of her last weeks in New York City, and it was also there that she was able to find the place that has remained her true home.

That place is a small cabin in the mountains, located about 12 miles (19 kilometers) from her high school. When she found it, it was love at first sight. "I walked into the

Rachael Ray tops her meatloaf with sauce in the kitchen of her cabin in Lake Luzerne, New York. When Ray moved back upstate after leaving New York City, she fell in love with this small cabin in the mountains. Though she owns the cabin now, she had trouble back then meeting the $575-a-month rent.

living room of the cabin," she told the Food Network's *Chefography*, "and I just knew. Like when you meet somebody that you want to marry . . . mentally it was a big hug."[1] At a rent-to-own cost of $575 a month, it put a considerable strain on her budget, but she knew that she had to live there. Ray, her mother, and from time to time her younger brother, Emmanuel, would make the place their home. The cabin was a place where Ray felt happy, safe, and secure. Now, all she really needed was a job that would use her abilities and love of food to the utmost.

NEW JOB/NEW CHALLENGES

She received a phone call in 1995 from Cowan & Lobel, a gourmet market in Albany, New York. The store needed a new food buyer and wanted to hire Ray. She wanted to take the position, but there was one problem. To work in Albany and still live in her beloved cabin, she would have to drive to and from work every day. Eager to take the job, she bit the bullet and did what she had long sworn that she would never do. She took a class and learned how to drive in three weeks, and, for the first time in her life, at the age of 27, she had her driver's license.

Driving, however, was still an uncomfortable experience for her. On her first day, she drove to work white-knuckled from gripping the steering wheel so hard, and then, on the drive home, she was pulled over by a policeman. She was driving with her high-beam headlights on. It turned out that she did not know what "high-beams" were, and the truck was still so new to her that she did not even know how to turn them off.

Gaining confidence in her driving skills was just one difficulty that Ray had upon starting her new job. Despite her friendly, cheerful attitude, some of her new co-workers thought that she was a bit of a "know it all" regarding food. In one incident, she and another employee, Vicki Filiaci, got into a screaming argument about whether sugar should be added to vinegar when making caponata, a Sicilian side dish composed of eggplant flavored with onion, tomatoes, anchovies, olives, pine nuts, capers, vinegar, and olive oil. Finally Ray broke the tension by exclaiming, "Vicki, it's only eggplant!"[2]

The two were soon fast friends, and Ray quickly ingratiated herself with the rest of the store's employees. (But it was Ray who got the last word on the caponata controversy. In her recipe for caponata, published in her first cookbook *30-Minute Meals*, she points out in the notes that "many recipes for caponata include sugar and/or vinegar; this is not one of them. My gran'pa Emmanuel said that the sweet and sour come out of the ingredients naturally."[3]) It was while working at Cowan & Lobel that Ray's talents truly blossomed. As Filiaci told *Vanity Fair*, "She was a workaholic back then as well. Her first holiday there, I mean the store was just amazing. It had never looked so good, and we'd never had so many cool things for our holiday. She bought it all, she put it all out, and it was just gorgeous stuff."[4]

Ray loved her work and the demands that her job put on her. In September 1996, she added even more responsibilities to her heavy workload. The prepared-foods chef, the person responsible for cooking the takeout dishes, suddenly quit, and Ray stepped in to help until a new chef could be hired. Her creations were so delicious and sold so well that the company asked her if she could be the food buyer *and* the prepared-foods chef. Ray was glad to oblige.

There was one problem, though. While Ray's prepared foods were selling well, the sales of groceries and gourmet food items were disappointing. Ray and the store's owners wondered what the problem was. Ray was an excellent buyer, and she was bringing in interesting, high-quality items—why weren't they selling?

Ray began to talk to the customers, trying to find out why they weren't buying products she felt they would love. The answer, it turned out, was simple. The customers were interested in the new gourmet products but did not know how to use them, and, perhaps equally important, did not feel that they really had time to cook. Faced with this problem, Ray, Filiaci, and bosses Jay and Donna Carnevale (Donna's family owned the store) sat down to figure out how to solve it. The solution, everybody felt, was a simple one: show people how to use the products, and then they will buy them. The decision was made to offer cooking classes to their customers.

But how could the classes be marketed? At the time, Domino's Pizza was in the middle of an advertising campaign promising that its pizzas would be delivered in 30 minutes or less. This gave Ray an idea, as she told *Vanity Fair*, "If people will wait 30 minutes for a pizza, they'd take 30 minutes to cook dinner. We'll sell gift certificates for a cooking class, we'll find a chef [to teach the class], and we'll call them '30-Minute Meals.'"[5] And so the concept of the 30-Minute Meal was born.

The idea was a good one, and sales for the gift certificates were even higher than expected. There was, however, one small snag in Ray's idea. Local chefs were either too busy or wanted too much money to teach the class. Who then was going to teach it?

The answer was obvious. Donna Carnevale suggested to Ray that she teach the class herself. While Ray protested that she was not a chef, Carnevale was not taking "no" for an answer, pointing out that the customers were already eating her prepared foods and loving them. So, clearly, while Ray may not have been a trained chef, she obviously knew how to cook food that people liked. The assignment was hers, and she set out planning how to do it, as she told Beverly Keel for *American Profile*:

We started the class and I made a packet of 30 30-minute Mediterranean meals because the best sellers every day were the pasta and chicken dishes. The class was three hours, and I would teach six basic recipes and five versions of what to do with each dish, so in that three hours you could really learn 30 30-minute meals. I taught the same things that I teach on my show, and that's how it started.[6]

With work stations set up in the store's kitchen, Ray would teach people how to use new ingredients that they might have been unfamiliar with. But, although she was a terrific teacher, she was not, as she has always pointed out, a trained chef. As she said on *Chefography*, "I'd teach people how to hack at an onion, which is completely incorrect, by the way. The way I chop onions is not the way you'd learn if you went to a gourmet cooking school."[7] Regardless of her technique or lack thereof, the onions got chopped, the food got cooked in 30 minutes, and customers learned how to use a growing array of "gourmet" food products. The cooking classes were a hit. As Ray told *Newsweek*, "It had this huge instant following. We had everyone from Girl Scouts and people getting married, to football players and retirees. It became this Wednesday-night thing."[8] The 30-Minute Meals, and Ray herself, began to gain attention from the local media.

BECOMING A LOCAL CELEBRITY

One day, reporter Dan Dinicola from the Albany TV station WRGB called Donna Carnevale and said, "You can't teach me how to cook in 30 minutes because I don't know how to cook."[9] Carnevale told him to get right over to the store, because a cooking class was going to start. Dinicola did come to the store, accompanied by a camera crew. He filmed the class, and, of course, to his apparent amazement, Ray did teach him how to cook a meal in just 30 minutes.

The segment was a hit, and Ray soon began to appear on regular cooking segments with Dinicola, which quickly became her own solo segment, "The 30-Minute Meal with Rachael Ray." Ray, while excited to be on television, was still happy working at Cowan & Lobel (it was this job that paid the bills), until a personnel shakeup in late 1997 forced her to reconsider her position there. A family disagreement forced Donna Carnevale, Ray's boss and friend, to leave the store. And, as Carnevale recounted to *Vanity Fair*, "Rachael said, 'If I don't work for you, I'm not going to work here.' She's extremely loyal—beyond. Loyalty to a fault. She had no job lined up. Nothing. She just left."[10]

MAKING ENDS MEET

Ray soon found work doing 30-Minute Meal demonstrations at local Price Chopper stores, while continuing her weekly cooking class on the WRGB local news. Even for a confirmed workaholic like Ray, it was a tremendous amount of work.

For the 30-Minute Meal demos, Ray would spend her day on the road, traveling from one Price Chopper store to another throughout upstate New York. As she described it on *Chefography*:

> I had a thing that looked like an Easy Bake Oven on steroids. It said "Rachael Ray's 30-Minute Meals," and I'd hand out these packets and recipes and I'd stand in the grocery store all day with two little burners and a countertop and I'd teach people how to make 30-Minute Meals.[11]

While the pay for the cooking demonstrations was poor, they still brought in more than her weekly cooking classes on television, which netted her only $50 a segment, despite

Along with her pit bull Isaboo, Rachael Ray attended the North Shore Animal League America's second annual DogCatemy Awards in November 2007 in New York City. Ray has had two pit bulls—the first was Boo, and then came Isaboo.

winning two local Emmy awards. (Ray would often end up spending her own money on the shows to make them more interesting.) In an effort to help her out financially, the news director at the time, Joe Coscia, had her start to do travel segments on the news called "Home and Away," which showed how to make travel fun, accessible, and affordable. He also put together demo tapes of her cooking segments and sent them to other local news directors throughout the country. The hope was that these news directors would want to purchase them to show on their own stations, which would, in turn make Ray some additional money. But no such luck. Ray was still just a local person from a small TV station in upstate New York. Why would anyone else in the country want to watch?

Even though Ray had no budget to speak of and production standards were relatively low, appearing on

IN HER OWN WORDS

Rachael Ray has had two pit bulls, Boo and Isaboo. During an interview with CNN's Larry King, he asked Ray what we don't know about pit bulls. She said:

> They're some of the sweetest animals on earth. I mean they're just like people. They can't . . . nothing can be born evil, not in my book anyway, and Boo was afraid of her own voice. If she would bark too loud, she'd run and hide under the sofa and I'd have to coax her out with treats. And Isaboo is wonderful with small children, and they're both very good eaters and they both love butternut squash.

the local news was a great learning experience for her. Working unscripted, and often going into people's homes to cook, Ray became comfortable working in television, showing an ease with teaching as well as an ability to be herself in front of a camera. In the face of the obvious limitations of local news, it was apparent that Ray had a natural sense of what looked good on television and how to present it.

Despite filming two local news segments, becoming something of a local celebrity, and working constantly demonstrating 30-Minute Meals at Price Chopper food stores, Ray often found it hard to make ends meet, and she often struggled just to pay the rent on the cabin. "We weren't living hand to mouth, but we were paycheck to paycheck," Ray told *Good Housekeeping*.[12] Still, Ray was happy doing what she was doing, and she, her mom, and her beloved pit bull Boo lived happily in her cabin, and had high hopes that prospects would get better.

GETTING PUBLISHED

By the end of 1998, Ray was ready to add one more project to her already hectic schedule. She and her mother often talked about her grandfather, now deceased, and his cooking. One way to keep his memory alive, they decided, was to write down his favorite recipes and make a book out of them. Those recipes, combined with Ray's initial group of 30-Minute Meal recipes, were soon collected and organized. Now all Ray would need was a publisher.

Knowing that one of the so-called major publishers would probably not be interested in her book, Ray contacted the small New York City publisher Lake Isle Press, headed by Hiroko Kiiffner. Kiiffner was at first reluctant to get involved in the project, feeling that a cookbook of 30-Minute Meals was not quite "sexy enough"[13] to make it in the marketplace. Not willing to take "no" for an answer,

Ray asked if she could come into the city and meet Kiiffner in person to discuss the book further.

Kiiffner agreed, and when Ray arrived at her office, she dumped a huge pile of recipes on her desk and asked for her help. Kiiffner was bowled over by both the recipes and Ray's personality and decided to publish the cookbook. (It also helped in her decision-making process that Price Chopper had promised to carry the cookbook in all of its New York stores.) Pleased that her book would be published, Ray had one more favor to ask. It was now August 1998. Would it be possible for the book to come out in time for Christmas?

Under normal circumstances, such a request would be impossible. Months, sometimes years go into the publishing of a book. Once again, though, Ray was unwilling to accept the possibility of failure. And somehow, some way, the book was published in time to be available for sale for Christmas 1998.

The book was an immediate success, selling all 10,000 copies of its first printing in just two weeks. Three months later, the book went into a second printing. For Ray, the cookbook was a turning point, as she wrote in *Newsweek*:

> That was the biggest achievement in my life at that point. I remember my mom and I got the check in January and we danced through the streets and just thought it was the most money in the world ever. We went to a really great restaurant and bought nice dresses for ourselves and had the best time.[14]

(Lake Isle Press would go on to publish Ray's first nine cookbooks. At that point in her career, her agents at William Morris urged Ray to move to the much larger publishing house of Clarkson Potter. Ray agreed to do so, but only if Lake Isle and Hiroko Kiiffner retained control of the nine titles that she had published. The professional

In May 2008, Rachael Ray signed copies of *Yum-O: The Family Cookbook* at a Barnes & Noble on the Upper West Side of Manhattan. *Yum-O* was Ray's fifteenth book since the debut in late 1998 of her first book, *30-Minute Meals*.

break was hard for both women, as Kiiffner told *The New York Times*: "When it's your baby and you've sort of nurtured it from the beginning, of course it's painful. We both acknowledged that our friendship and personal relationship were more important."[15])

With two continuing news segments and a successful, locally sold cookbook, Ray had gone just about as far as she could in her career while remaining in upstate New York. Now all she would need was a break, something that could bring her to the attention of a national audience. Although all she needed was one break, she was about to receive two—changing her life and her career forever.

A Food Network
Star Is Born

Break number one. On March 2, 2001, a blizzard was threatening to hit New York City. The *Today* show, NBC's popular morning news and entertainment program, was facing the cancellation of scheduled guests who would not be able to make it to the city because of the expected storm. Al Roker, the show's popular weatherman and host, who has a house in upstate New York, had seen Rachael Ray on television and thought that she might make an ideal substitute guest. That day, Ray's mom received a phone call at the cabin from the show's producer, Michele Leone, saying that *Today* wanted to put Ray on the show but would need a decision that day. Elsa promised to find her daughter and have her call back as soon as possible.

Ray was working at a Price Chopper when she got the call from her mother. At first she could not believe that *Today* would be calling her and thought one of her friends was pulling a prank. Wary, she called back the number that her mother gave her, but when the person on the line answered "*Today* show," Ray freaked out so badly that she immediately hung up the phone, took a deep breath, and then called back. Would it be possible, the show's producer asked, for Ray to come into New York and make four different hearty winter soups for Al Roker? Ray, not believing her good luck, immediately said yes and quickly raced home to begin to pack up the car with everything she would need. Fortunately for her, she was already scheduled to be in New York City the day after her appearance on *Today*, which leads us to:

Break number two. Just days before Ray received her phone call from the *Today* show, a man named Lou Ekus had been driving through upstate New York and had heard her teach a class on how to cook jambalaya over the radio. (How someone can teach cooking over the radio is another matter altogether.) Ekus called his good friend Bob Tuschman, senior vice president of programming at the Food Network, and told him that he should definitely check out Ray. Of course, since Ekus had only *heard* Ray, he had no idea if she was young or old, or even what she looked like. Tuschman immediately went out to find a copy of Ray's cookbook, and after seeing her picture, he knew at least that she would look good on television. He called to set up an appointment for a meeting.

MAKING IT TO THE BIG TIME

One can only imagine what must have been racing through Ray's mind as she and her mom made the drive to New York City, with two major, possibly career-defining events

Rachael Ray shared some Thanksgiving tips and some laughs with Al Roker during an appearance on November 22, 2005, on the *Today* show. Four years earlier, Roker had seen Ray's local "30-Minute Meal" spots and had suggested to *Today*'s producers that she would make a great substitute guest.

coming up within the next 48 hours. But first things first, and their top priority was to make it to New York City alive and in one piece.

The predicted snowstorm had hit the northeastern United States with a vengeance, and there was almost four feet of snow on the ground when Rachael and Elsa set out on their journey, making it nearly impossible to drive. The trip, which normally took no more than four hours, stretched out to nearly seven hours. By the time Ray made it to the studios, she only had 70 minutes to prepare her four soups. In fact, she was still cooking while they were putting on her makeup. And, of course, Ray still had doubts as to her qualifications for cooking on *Today*. "I was like, 'What am I doing here? I am a waitress from upstate New York. What qualification do I have to be showing all of America how to make soup?" she is quoted as saying.[1]

Once she made it on the air, though, the segment went smoothly. (Although, because of a slight case of nerves, she did say the word "groovy" several more times than was really necessary.) Ray herself was pleased with how the show went, saying on *Chefography* that:

> I made it through, everybody loved the food, and nobody died. Al hugged me, and everybody was eating, and it was like a choir of angels opened up and the heavens shined down upon us and somehow everything was OK.[2]

And, in a lucky break for Ray, because of the blizzard, it seemed as though everybody in the Northeast who was stuck at home was watching her, giving her by far her largest audience to date. Among those watching was Bob Tuschman of the Food Network, who said that "I watched her on the *Today* show and she was astounding. She grabbed the camera, she lit up the screen, she was fun, not polished, but fun."[3] Based on her performance, Tuschman was even more confident that Rachael Ray and the Food Network would be a perfect fit.

She would, however, be a different kind of chef and television personality than the Food Network had ever hired, as Tuschman explained to the television show *Biography*:

> Before Rachael came to us, we were a channel of mostly rather high-end restaurant chefs, cooking

kind of upscale food that a lot of people loved
watching but probably weren't really going to make.
So when Rachael came, she thought she was coming
to the wrong place.[4]

And it is true that the Food Network, which debuted
on cable on November 23, 1993, as a response to America's
growing love and fascination for fine food and cooking,
had begun by presenting restaurant-quality food for home
kitchens. Chefs like Mario Batali, Bobby Flay, and Emeril
Lagasse, who were among the network's biggest stars, were
highly trained chefs whose restaurants were considered
to be among the best in the country. Even Sara Moulton,
whose show *Cooking Live!* was in some ways a precursor to
30-Minute Meals, was a graduate of the prestigious Culinary
Institute of America and executive chef of *Gourmet* magazine. In many ways, the Food Network of 2001 *was* out of
Ray's league.

Ray herself was the first to admit that, as she con-
fessed to *Biography*. At the beginning of the meeting with
Tuschman, "I just blurted out . . . You don't want to give me
a job here. I'm not a chef. There's been some kind of mis-
understanding. I'm grossly unqualified. You're champagne;
I'm beer out of a bottle."[5] She then got up to leave but
stopped dead in her tracks when she was told, "No, no, no,
stop. That's what we like. We don't want you to be a chef."[6]
She was signed to do 25 episodes of *30-Minute Meals* and
40 episodes of *$40 a Day* (a budget travel show, similar to
her local-news segment "Home and Away"). Despite Ray's
doubts, the Food Network was convinced that she had all
the makings of a star, as Tuschman explained in a Food
Network documentary:

What she didn't know is that we loved her precisely
because she was very unlike the chefs on our

channel. She was down to earth. She was accessible. She wasn't restaurant trained, she was home trained. But she spoke and cooked like a home cook did, and that's what was so appealing to us.[7]

Without question, Ray had come along with the right idea at the right time, as Brooke Johnson, president of the Food Network, believed:

> Cooking used to be hours and hours in the kitchen, and obviously, with the number of working women in this country, they don't have time to do it. Rachael figured that out and gave it a great name; really fun, interesting ingredients; ways to mix and match—just things you wouldn't think of.[8]

Ray's appeal, though, went beyond the food, Johnson continued:

> She's got a big, big, personality. She doesn't hide from you, and that's very attractive to people. She has a vulnerability, because she's so open. That's part of her charisma. And she has tremendous energy. She jumps off the screen.[9]

30-MINUTE MEALS

Her show *30-Minute Meals* debuted on the Food Network on November 2, 2001. It is obvious from watching her early shows that she was still a little nervous, still working out a way to become "Rachael Ray" on camera. It did not take long, however, for her to reach her stride, as Bob Tuschman described in Ray's Food Network biography:

> She was good. She started out at a good level. But she was tentative. She's not the big Rachael that you

know. She was a little quieter, a little softer, a little shyer. There was a learning curve, but it's a short one. Rachael is one of the fastest learners on the face of the planet.[10]

But even if Ray was a fast learner, there were still mistakes made, both in rehearsal and while shooting the show. Used to working on a shoestring budget, Ray was initially unaccustomed to having assistants set up and prepare her kitchen. Walking onto the set one day, she poured olive oil into a sauté pan, not realizing that someone had already turned on the burner and that the pan was, as Ray would put it, "screaming hot." The oil burst into flames, and Ray nearly burst into tears, wondering if she was ready for the big time.

She was. The show was an immediate hit, quickly becoming one of the Food Network's most popular programs. The audience liked her ability to laugh at her own mistakes—for example, while filming the first episode, she cut off the tip of her finger, which had to be Krazy Glued back on. That quality, Ray's girl-next-door appeal and, of course, her food combined to make a nearly irresistible package for Food Network viewers.

Not everyone, however, saw her appeal. Many of the Food Network stars at the time, trained professional chefs, were dismayed that they were on the same channel as Ray. After all, she was not trained, she did not teach classical techniques, and she was not ashamed to use pre-packaged ingredients. As one insider to the world of food told *Vanity Fair*, "Rachael Ray comes along as an enthusiastic amateur, and some people in the food firmament bemoan it."[11]

To all of these criticisms, Ray was in complete agreement. "I can't debate anything they have to say about me," she said. "I am not a chef. I don't know how to

Rachael Ray poses in a publicity shot for *30-Minute Meals* a couple of months before the show's November 2001 debut on the Food Network. One network executive said that Ray was a bit shy at first but soon found her comfort level on the program.

bake. I do use store-bought pierogi. I didn't make my own pierogi. I don't need to make the dumpling to feel fulfilled."[12]

What did fulfill Ray was work and lots of it. Along with *30-Miniute Meals*, Ray was also filming *$40 a Day*, the Food Network's entry into the world of travel shows. She described the show's genesis and the meeting at which it was discussed (Ray's first meeting with the Food Network) on *Larry King Live*:

> Under $40 was actually a hybrid of a show that Food Network was working on—a concept I think they were going to call "Rich Man, Poor Man" and they were going to give one guy like $500 and another guy $50 and see what they did with each. And I just gave them an opinion because we were also doing budget travel on the local news upstate by then.
>
> I said, "You know, I got to tell you, I've been waiting on wealthy people all my life and there isn't anybody that doesn't like a good bargain." So, I think the bargain show was going to be really killer and they offered it to me, too, so I ended up with two shows.[13]

This meeting shows Ray at her best. Even though it was her first interview with the Food Network, she was not afraid to disagree with management and she did not hesitate to say what *she* thought would make the show successful, incorporating lifelong lessons in thriftiness learned from her mother. Ray was convinced that no one would really care how the rich traveled, but that everyone, rich and poor, would have more fun and get more enjoyment out of traveling on a budget.

Initially, though, the show was not a success; but it did eventually take off, becoming another hit for Ray. But hit or not, Ray had the time of her life filming the series. She loved traveling and relished the opportunity to introduce America to what she saw as "poor guy" travel spots. And again, as with *30-Minute Meals*, it was Ray's persona and the fact that she was not your typical travel host that made the show so successful. She giggled, she screamed when attacked by seagulls while eating along the coast—she obviously *enjoyed* herself and her travels on camera, and *that* is what viewers responded to.

As for Ray, who had always wanted to travel but could rarely afford to, the show was the opportunity of her life, allowing her to go places she had never been and to subsequently share some of her favorite places with her viewers, places like Tuscany, Italy. The show also allowed her to try her hand at a variety of activities: waterskiing, trapeze, and an activity that has since become one of her favorites—skydiving. As she told *Chefography*, the thrill of skydiving allows you to "put all of your ducks in a row rather quickly. It quiets you. Short of a lobotomy, it's the best thing for me."[14]

WHAT IS A 30-MINUTE MEAL?

Although Ray loved doing *$40 a Day*, she knew that *30-Minute Meals* was her trademark, her meat and potatoes. It was what had gotten her her start, what sold cookbooks, what got her the attention of the Food Network. All of

DID YOU KNOW?

Did you know that among Rachael Ray's many television appearances, she is particularly proud of being on *Sesame Street*? It's true! In 2007, during the show's thirty-eighth season, Ray appeared in an episode to present "pumpernickel" as the word of the day. (Pumpernickel is a dark German bread made of rye flour and coarsely ground rye meal.)

which raises an important question: What exactly is a 30-Minute Meal?

Obviously, the idea of getting dinner quickly on the table did not originate with Ray. Frozen foods and prepackaged food like Hamburger Helper were designed to help harried housewives get a hot dinner on the table quickly and easily. The writer Peg Bracken had a popular success in 1960 with *The I Hate to Cook Book*, which mocked the beginnings of the gourmet food revolution and encouraged housewives to use as many convenience foods as possible. Later, in the 1980s, *The New York Times* struck a chord with the weekly column *The 60-Minute Gourmet* by Pierre Franey, which later became a series of highly successful cookbooks. Unlike Ray's 30-Minute Meals, though, Franey did not simplify the recipes by taking shortcuts and using prepackaged ingredients: His goal was to show that classic French dishes (along with other cuisines) were not all time-consuming and labor-intensive and that many could actually be made in as little as 60 minutes. For many foodies who came of age in the 1980s, *The 60-Minute Gourmet* cookbooks were as dog-eared and food-stained as Ray's cookbooks are today.

But what Ray does with her 30-Minute Meals is different in approach from what Franey did. She can take almost any recipe, no matter how complicated it may be in its original form, and adapt it to a 30-minute format (or as she calls it, "canoodling" the recipe). She will streamline the recipe, simplify the techniques, change the ingredients to make the recipe more accessible and affordable, and lay it all out so it can be cooked within 30 minutes. Let's look at how she does it, for example, with a classic Italian dish, pasta Bolognese.

Pasta Bolognese is a favorite Italian specialty of pasta, traditionally the long, broad noodles known as tagliatelle, tossed with meat sauce, of which there are nearly as many recipes as there are chefs who make them (although the basic concept of the traditional sauce remains the same). In her book *Essentials of Classic Italian Cooking*, Marcella Hazan, the woman who helped to introduce authentic Italian food to America and who is considered by many foodies to be "the Italian Julia Child," laid out her version, a recipe that is widely considered to be definitive.

The recipe begins by slowly sautéing finely chopped onion, celery, and carrots in a mixture of oil and butter. Ground chuck is added, and gently cooked and crumbled into small pieces, along with salt and pepper. Milk is added to the meat/vegetable mixture and allowed to simmer gently until it bubbles away completely. A bit of nutmeg is added, then white wine, which is also allowed to simmer until it has evaporated. At that stage, cut-up tomatoes are added, and the sauce cooks, barely bubbling, for at least three hours, preferably more. The completed sauce is tossed with pasta and butter, and served with grated Parmesan cheese on the side. The dish, by any standards, is magnificent.

In Ray's version, ground meat is sautéed over medium high heat. Garlic, crushed red pepper, and allspice (her family's secret ingredient) are added, along with grated onion. The mixture is allowed to cook for a few minutes; beef broth and red wine are added, along with crushed tomatoes and parsley. The sauce simmers for the amount of time it takes to make pasta (if the pasta water is already boiling—less than 10 minutes). The sauce is then tossed with the pasta, and Parmesan cheese is served on the side. Is it delicious? Of course. Is it a true sauce Bolognese? Probably not. Does it matter?

So when looking at both recipes, in what ways are they different? What changes did Ray make? How did she "canoodle it" to make it a 30-Minute Meal? Time, obviously, is a huge difference between the two. Hazan's recipe would probably take 30 to 40 minutes of preparation before it gets to the long, slow three-to-four-hour simmer. Ray's

Marcella Hazan, who helped to introduce authentic Italian cooking to Americans, peels some red and yellow peppers for one of her signature dishes. Hazan's classic recipe for pasta Bolognese takes three to four hours to prepare. Rachael Ray's adaptation, with a few shortcuts and substitutions, takes a half-hour.

version would be finished and on the table before Hazan's version had even started simmering. There are other differences as well. Hazan's traditional technique of simmering the meat in milk is gone from Ray's version. While Hazan calls specifically for one cup of white wine, Ray calls for "two glugs" (about ⅓ cup) of red wine. Are both recipes good? Certainly. Is Hazan's a "true" Bolognese, the real thing, in comparison with Ray's version? Yes. Her sauce has a depth of flavor, a richness, a complexity of taste that only long, careful cooking can provide. On the other hand, and this question is important when comparing the two recipes which sauce is someone more likely to make for his or her family after a full day of work? The answer is obvious.

And that, in a nutshell, is what makes Rachael Ray's 30-Minute Meals so successful. By taking classic recipes and streamlining them so that anyone can make them after a long day, she turns cooking into something that people can do, and most important, *want* to do. By making recipes less intimidating to home cooks, by putting aside precise measurements (they take time after all!) for general concepts such as "a few glugs" or "a couple of handfuls," she puts the "fun" back into cooking.

Don't have time to make paella, a classic, labor-intensive Spanish dish of seafood, chicken, sausage and rice? Use ground chicken, sausage and shrimp and make paella burgers instead! Think you don't have time to make soup? In 15 minutes, not much longer than it takes to open a can of soup and heat it, you can make "My Mom's 15-Minute Tomato and Bean Stoup." (In Rachael-speak, "stoup" is a dish that's thicker than a soup, thinner than a stew.) Ray makes good-tasting, healthy food available to everyone, no matter how much time they have.

Before, home cooks who wanted to prepare the new and exciting dishes they were reading about or watching on television might have felt intimidated. Ray, however, has a way of making the idea seem far less frightening. One way she makes cooking less intimidating is by avoiding the use of hard-to-find specialty ingredients. The logic is: Who's going to cook a 30-minute meal if they have to spend hours going to specialty markets trying to find the ingredients a recipe requires? Indeed, Ray has vowed never to write a recipe with an ingredient that she cannot find at the local Price Chopper. If she can find it there, she feels, anyone can find it anywhere.

On her show and in her cookbooks, Ray takes the time to discuss the use of ingredients that some people may be unfamiliar with and describe what they taste like. Then she goes a step further and tells viewers where exactly in the store they can find the ingredients. If people can easily find the products, without having to go to the hassle or embarrassment of asking someone at the store, they are much more likely to use the ingredients.

Ray has one more rule to make the whole idea of 30-Minute Meals more accessible and affordable, as she explained in *Vanity Fair*. "I won't allow the books to be pricier than a music CD. Because they're collections of everything that I do on-air, and I just feel you shouldn't be paying more than you would for a popular song. I consider my food the equivalent of a pop song."[15]

By making the preparation of good food seem less intimidating and more affordable, people are more comfortable with cooking and eating new foods. With 30-minute recipes for dishes like "Lime-and-Honey Glazed Salmon with Warm Black Bean and Corn Salad," "Chicken in Spicy and Sweet Onion Sauce with Goat Cheese Smashed Potatoes and a Watercress and Cucumber Salad," "Indian Tofu and Spinach over Almond Rice," and "Chorizo and Butternut Soup with Herbed Tomato and Cheese Quesadillas," Ray brings the resultant rewards of the American food revolution to the home cook.

In retrospect, the concept of 30-Minute Meals seems obvious, but as its creator, Ray was the one to reap the rewards. Her first contract with the Food Network, for 25 episodes of *30-Minute Meals* and 40 episodes of *$40 a Day*, paid her what she considered the astronomical sum of $360,000. The first thing she did with the money? For many people the first purchase they would make after signing such a large contract would be a new, expensive car. But not Ray. The first thing she did was to reupholster the old family furniture in her upstate cabin. The second thing she did? Buy the cabin. For Ray, thriftiness and practicality are a permanent part of her personality. As she told *Redbook*:

> If somebody handed me a check for $2 million tomorrow and said you can't keep this unless you go and spend it all in one day, then I'd probably give it back. Because I think that in everything in life, there's a limit for me. Shoes I'll spend a couple of hundred—I would never spend . . . I mean they have shoes out there that cost $1,200 to $1,500 for a pair of shoes! I mean, no matter what the category is, there's always something. There's a limit for me with everything. . . . I'm not about poor or cheap or being thrifty, but I am about value. I don't mind spending more money on something as long as I know the intrinsic value of that thing. For me, it's always more about quality than about the price point.[16]

As her career took off and she achieved a level of financial security, Ray was thrilled to be able to buy the cabin she had considered home for so long. It seems unlikely that she could possibly have imagined that her career was really beginning and that the time she would be able to spend in her cabin would become more and more limited.

She Never Stops

While Rachael Ray had always been industrious, she was entering a period of nonstop work that made her earlier life look like a life of leisure. Filming *30-Minute Meals* in New York City, traveling the world to shoot *$40 a Day*, writing cookbooks, making personal appearances throughout the country, Ray experienced an endless whirl of activity. This, of course, is how she prefers it, as she told *Redbook* magazine:

> I can't really sit idle. I don't mind if it's a rainy day watching TV all day in bed with my dog. That's fun. But generally speaking, unless it's pouring rain outside, or unless I'm really, really sick, it freaks me out to kind of be still. The best I can do is write when

I go on vacation, which is a fairly quiet activity. I'll write the books or recipes or whatever.[1]

She was, in essence, living the life she had always dreamed of having. But one thing was missing. Constantly busy, constantly on the run, Ray did not have the time for friends and a personal life. And she certainly did not have the time for a boyfriend. Or so she thought.

FINDING LOVE

Ray's best friends have always been her family—her mother, Elsa, whom she lovingly calls "Mamacello," has been her very best friend from the time she was a little girl. Working as hard as she does makes it difficult for Ray to maintain relationships, as she told *Redbook*:

> I never had a ton of girlfriends or boyfriends 'cause I work a lot. I always have. And some of my closest friends I work with, so we see each other when I'm at work, and, you know, I've got a couple of friends from back in the day. We really just talk on the phone once every few months and we see each other maybe once or twice a year 'cause I just work a ton.[2]

Can you imagine being so driven to work that you barely have time to maintain friendships?

So, if time for friends was severely limited, the time for a boyfriend was nearly nonexistent. It's not that Ray didn't have boyfriends over the years. How could anyone with her intelligence, looks, and personality not have boyfriends? But there was never a relationship that lasted. She explained on *Biography* that "the little bit of freedom that I had I wanted to be with my family. The guys wanted a little bit of just guy time, time with themselves, and I'm just not equipped to give it to them."[3] To find herself in a relationship, she would have to find a man who would be willing to take her on her own terms. He would have to be a man who wanted an independent woman, a man who was confident and secure enough about himself not to be intimidated by her growing fame. She would find the man she would eventually marry in late 2001.

His name was John Cusimano, an entertainment lawyer, film distributor, and lead singer and guitarist for the punk band The Cringe. Ray told Larry King in an interview how they met:

> That's a funny story. Well, we had an acquaintance who recommended us to each other, but because this person was really racy and out on the town and very, you know, kind of a jet-set type, we thought, oh jeez, a friend of that person wouldn't like me. And he thought the same. Then we went to a party that person threw. Everybody there was really tall except me and John, so we saw each other right away.[4]

As Cusimano elaborated, "We saw each other in a sea of knees."[5] The person having the party bent down to Ray and said, "Hey, dummy, that's the guy I wanted you to meet a year ago."[6]

There was, for both of them, an immediate attraction. Ray described it as: "We've been plastered on each other, making people sick ever since then."[7] Cusimano remembers that "my very good friend who was with me and single at the time, you know how single guys never want their other single friends hooked up, he looked at me and goes, oh, you are done."[8] Cusimano agreed, thinking to himself during that first encounter that she could be the one. And indeed, ever since that party, the two have been together.

Rachael Ray and her husband, John Cusimano *(right)*, watched the band Scissors for Lefty perform in March 2008 at the SXSW Music Festival in Austin, Texas. Cusimano, who is an entertainment lawyer, is also the lead singer and guitarist for the punk band The Cringe.

Both short and Italian, the two were initially brought together by a mutual love of food and music. At their first meeting, Ray tested him on his food acumen, and he passed with flying colors, as she told Knight Ridder Newspapers: "A big line guys use with me is 'I can cook.' So I always asked them, 'OK, so what did you make last night?' Ninety percent of them say chili. John told me he cooked tilapia (a mild-tasting fish) with tomatillo and a maque choux—a Cajun dish of corn, cream, bell peppers, and tomatoes. He had me at tilapia."[9]

Their relationship quickly deepened, going beyond a mutual love of food, and the couple fell in love and became each other's best friends. As Cusimano explained in a documentary on Ray's life on *Biography*, "She's my buddy. She's the person I want to talk to about everything. Nothing really seems real . . . until she knows about it and vice versa. If you're living with your best friend, life is great."[10]

As for Ray, she had found the one man who could easily live with her celebrity, her need for hard work, and her independent streak. "I'm a lousy girlfriend, and I think for every other guy on the planet I would be a lousy wife. For my husband, it's like breathing," she told *Biography*.[11] Ray elaborated by telling *People* magazine that "I can't give a man an enormous amount of attention. And John is totally down with that. When men I have dated over the years whined about, 'Oh, you make no time for me'—see ya! I just dumped them. I don't need that pressure in my life."[12]

With Cusimano, though, that was not a problem. Busy with his own life and career, he and Ray seemed to be a perfect match—two people both looking for the same attributes in a spouse. After three years of dating, Cusimano got down on his knee to propose marriage. Ray was so excited at the

DID YOU KNOW?

Did you know that Rachael Ray loves to listen to music while she's cooking? Her taste ranges from rockers like Muse, the Foo Fighters, U2, and, of course, her husband John Cusimano's group The Cringe, to jazz musicians like Chet Baker, Louis Armstrong, and Keely Smith, to opera singers like Luciano Pavarotti.

prospect that she immediately started to scream at the top of her lungs, along with punching, tackling, and wrestling the surprised Cusimano. Ray's answer, despite the eruption of physical activity, was yes, although the relationship had come at a time when she had nearly given up on the idea of marriage. "He came at a point in my life when I had decided I'm not going to chase [marriage]," she told *People* magazine. "I don't think young men or women should feel pressured into marriage. You shouldn't marry anyone, in my opinion, who you have to try hard for."[13]

Still, even before the proposal, Ray knew that Cusimano was the man she was going to marry. How did she know? On his birthday, she asked him what he would like for his birthday dinner, offering to make lobster, steak, any food, any cuisine he wanted. Cusimano's response? "Can I just have some of your carbonara?"[14] Carbonara is a simple dish of pasta tossed with bacon, eggs, and parmesan cheese, the kind that Ray grew up eating. When Cusimano told her that carbonara was the dish he wanted most of all, she *knew* that he was the man she wanted to spend her life with.

The couple married on September 24, 2005, in Montalcino, Italy, in the region of Tuscany, long one of Ray's favorite spots on Earth. Why Montalcino? It turns out that the couple's favorite wine, Brunello, is made in the region. For two food- and wine-obsessed people in love, Montalcino seemed like the ideal location to say their vows.

The wedding took place in a castle, and the two were married surrounded by more than 130 of their closest friends and family members, whom Ray had flown to Italy to be part of the three-day wedding celebration. As a friend described the event on *Chefography*, "It sounds very upscale, high-faluting, but it really wasn't like that at all. It was a bunch of really lucky people who had an amazing friend who thought that she wanted to make her wedding not just special to her but to everyone that was around her."[15]

Ray's time was now split between her beloved cabin in the Adirondacks and a duplex in Manhattan's trendy Greenwich Village neighborhood. She stays in the city when she shoots her shows, while her mother lives full time in the cabin, where she answers Ray's fan mail, organizes her charity work, and works the land that surrounds the cabin. There, Elsa has created a beautiful Tuscan-style garden, complete with stone paths, fire pits, and even a bocce court. (Bocce is an Italian bowling-type game, played outdoors.) "This is what happens once a person retires and they've worked all their life and you leave them alone in the woods," Elsa told *The New York Times*.[16]

Although Ray enjoys her life in New York City, she has a rule that, whenever she has at least 36 hours off, she goes home upstate. It is, after all these years, still her favorite place to be, still the place where she feels most at home. She told *American Profile* that "I like being home. I like a cozy life. The sky is darker, the stars are brighter, and things make more sense to me when I'm in the middle of the woods. You can play your music as loud as you want and nobody bugs you."[17]

A LITTLE CONTROVERSY

As Rachael Ray's popularity grew, as *30-Minute Meals* and *$40 a Day* became more and more an essential part of Food Network programming, demand grew for Ray to appear on other television shows, to do newspaper interviews, and to appear in various magazines. One such request from a magazine turned out to cause a good amount of controversy, and to earn the strong disapproval of Ray's mother.

In 2003, the editors of *FHM* (For Him Magazine) contacted the publicity people at the Food Network and asked whether Ray would like to appear in their magazine. *FHM*, similar to *Maxim*, is a men's magazine that owes much of its popularity to photos of scantily clad women—a fact Ray initially was unaware of, thinking that 'FHM" stood for "Food and Housewares and . . ." When she found out the truth about the offer, her initial response was "How crazy is that?" Still, she was intrigued by the idea. After talking it over with Cusimano, she decided to do the photo shoot. She told *Biography* that "I always feel very troll-like, kind of like Frodo. I thought if I could be brave enough to do it, it would make me feel better about myself, my husband certainly wouldn't hate it, and I thought it would be good for women in general to see a woman who's over 35, who is a real person, in there among all that stuff."[18]

Many people, though, criticized her for cheapening her image in such photos. The pictures included Ray taking a turkey out of the oven wearing little more than a black bra, an extremely short gingham skirt, high heels and a smile, and Ray wearing short-shorts with a bare midriff, licking chocolate off a big wooden spoon. Ray's mother, a longtime feminist, was not at all pleased, pointing out that none of the men in the magazine were so exposed in *their* photos. Ray, though, did not care about the criticism, telling *Biography* that the photos were "tasteful, I'm proud of it, and I wouldn't take it back."[19] She added, in a *New York Times* interview, "When I'm 80 I'm going to look back and be like, 'I represented!' "[20]

POPULARITY AND CRITICISM

By the end of 2005, Ray's television shows were on the Food Network 13 hours a week. *30-Minute Meals* was still going strong and *$40 a Day* was still being shown, while *Tasty Travels* (her new travel show) and *Inside Dish* (Ray dines and talks with famous celebrities) were popular as well. To her many fans, who could not get enough of her, Ray had become *the* face of the Food Network.

Rachael Ray and some of her crew members visited a replica of the Oval Office at the Clinton Presidential Library in Little Rock, Arkansas. Ray was at the library in February 2006 to tape a segment for one of her new Food Network shows, *Tasty Travels*. At the time, she had four shows on the Food Network: *30-Minute Meals*, *$40 a Day*, *Tasty Travels*, and *Inside Dish*.

For others, though, her presence was just too much. It seemed that every time you turned on the Food Network, there she was. It seemed as if she was on the cover of every magazine. Everywhere you went, it seemed, there was Rachael Ray. And with her ever-growing popularity, there was an ever-increasing number of people ready and willing to make fun of, mock, and criticize everything about her.

Foodies made fun of the meals she cooked, criticizing her reliance on store-bought chicken broth and prepackaged items like cornbread mix. They claim that it's nearly impossible to make her meals in 30 minutes, especially for people with little experience in the kitchen. (Jill Hunter Pellettieri of *Slate*, even while defending Ray, said that she tried 21 recipes and was not able to complete a single one in just 30 minutes. The best she could do was a menu of Super Sloppy Joes, Deviled Potato Salad, and Root Beer Floats in 49 minutes and 51 seconds. And she skipped the root beer floats.)

Ray is the first to admit that she is not a trained chef, that her food isn't professional food, and that she is, as she always says, "completely unqualified for any job I've ever had."[21] Fellow Food Network chef and restaurant owner Mario Batali has become one of her strongest defenders, telling *Vanity Fair* that "she's very comfortable and very calm when she's cooking, coaxing people gently to get out of that fast-food and cheesy restaurant business and try to eat something they make at home."[22] As for why some big-name chefs do not like Ray? Batali attributes it to one simple thing: jealousy. "She has singlehandedly changed the entire cookbook market, and a lot of chefs aren't happy about that. Someone sells 50,000 copies of a book, it used to be considered very nice. Rachael's upped the ante. She's created a market where she can do two or three books in a year, and they'll all sell a million copies."[23]

(It's interesting to note that, if anyone should be jealous of Ray, it's Mario Batali. Doralece Dullaghan, director of promotions for Sur La Table, a gourmet store that carries Ray's line of knives and sauté pans, as well as her cookbooks, has said that, at book signings, Ray outdraws Batali by nearly two to one. Dullaghan went on to say that, unlike the calm crowd that comes to see Batali, Ray's audience members loudly cheer for her and come forward to tell her about their families, their vacations, and the dishes that they have cooked. Obviously, Ray's fans think of her as more than a television star—they see her as a friend.)

While criticisms of Ray's recipes and 30-Minute Meals may be fair game, her critics sometimes attack her on a more personal level. Even her defenders, such as Jill Hunter Pellettieri, admit that Ray's "ditzy demeanor also makes her easy to dismiss."[24] She *does* giggle constantly, she *does* make too much noise in the kitchen, and she *does* drop things

RACHAEL-ISMS

Love them or hate them, "Rachael-isms" have become one of Rachael Ray's trademarks. They are the abbreviations and cute names she uses when talking about food. "Rachael-speak" has become part of everyday language for many Americans—in fact, EVOO was recently accepted into the *Oxford American College Dictionary*. Here are some of the commonly used Rachael-isms:

- **EVOO**: An abbreviation for extra-virgin olive oil—the highest-quality olive oil available. As Ray says on her Web site, "I first coined 'EVOO' on my cooking show because saying 'extra-virgin olive oil' over and over was wordy, and I'm an impatient girl—that's why I make 30-minute meals!"*
- **Yum-O!**: Used when "yum" just isn't enough.
- **Delish!**: One step beyond Yum-O!
- **Two Turns of the Pan**: Instead of using measurements, let's say, for how much olive oil to use in a pan for cooking, Ray says to use enough to go two turns around the

while trying to carry too much from the fridge to the stove. And most grating to some people, she has her own vocabulary of "Rachael-isms," cutesy names for food such as "sammies" and "stoups."

Others go even further in their criticisms. There is a Web site, whose name is too crude to mention, created "for people that hate the untalented twit known as Rachael Ray."[25] There, the bloggers make fun of her smile, which they compare to that of the Joker in Batman comics. They

pan. That amount is the equivalent of about two table-spoons.
- **Eyeball It**: Another form of measurement, meaning you judge it with your eyes, not with a measuring spoon. When measuring spices, for example, the amount that fits into the palm of her hand is about one tablespoon.
- **Sammie**: A sandwich.
- **Stoup**: A dish that's thicker than a normal soup, yet thinner than a stew—a combination of the two words.
- **GH**: A grownup-helper, someone who acts as an assistant to young chefs, helping with heavy pots, boiling water, and other tasks that can be difficult or dangerous for cooks in training.
- **How Good Is That?**: Congratulate yourself on a well-cooked meal, sit down, and enjoy it!

---

*"Rachael-Isms." *Every Day with Rachael Ray* Web site. Available online at http://www.rachaelraymag.com/about-rachael/rachael-isms/article.html.

mock her voice, the way she dresses—they even get kicks out of calling her cruel names like "Retchel." Ray, though, takes it all in stride, even agreeing with most of those who may criticize her cooking, telling *Vanity Fair* that "most of what they say is absolutely true . . . [but] you can't be all things to all people."[26]

Of course, Ray has many more fans then detractors. For millions of viewers across the country, Ray makes cooking at home a reality. Ray is like them—making mistakes in the kitchen, far from perfect, but still able to get dinner on the table in 30 minutes. Ray, the girl-next-door, represents something attainable for the average (or even below-average) home cook. In this, she is different not only from the other chefs on the Food Network, but also from the other prominent female television chef of the era—Martha Stewart.

Stewart, the famous cookbook author, television personality, and multimedia mogul, represents something completely different from Ray. Stewart strives for perfection. Her recipes are complicated and time-consuming. She does not take shortcuts and does not use convenience items when cooking. She speaks quietly in hushed tones, using classical cooking terms and techniques, and is neatly dressed with never a hair out of place. While she represents an ideal, much of what she does is unattainable for the average cook.

Ray is, in many ways, the "anti-Martha." Her recipes are easy to prepare. She talks loudly and proudly shows her mistakes on camera. She doesn't use classical cooking terms: "shimmy-shake," "smokin'," and "screaming hot" are only are a few of the phrases she uses to describe her dishes. So if Stewart (along with other television chefs) represents a nearly impossible ideal, Ray represents the altogether possible. Television producer Aimee Baker spoke of the difference to *The New York Times*, saying "of course it never takes

At the 2006 South Beach Wine and Food Festival in Florida, Rachael Ray prepared a pasta dish for the audience. Some foodies criticize her reliance on store-bought items, but her many fans appreciate that Ray makes cooking at home a reality.

you 30 minutes, but I like the idea of it. She's so not stressful at all. I love those other TV chefs, but I would never make what Mario Batali makes. I don't have veal cheeks."[27]

As for Ray herself, she finds it hard to believe that she had even been compared with Martha Stewart, telling Larry King that:

> I've always felt terrible about that because Martha knows how to do so much more than Rachael Ray. I mean Martha knows how to craft and bake and build, you know. She is iconic. . . . I am a miserable failure at 90 percent of what Martha can do so beautifully well. And I've always thought it's a wonderful compliment for me to be compared on any level with Martha. And it must be very not-so-fun to have somebody who can barely make burgers and pasta, you know, compared with someone who's worked so hard and done so many things.[28]

The comparisons, though, were inevitable, and were soon to become even more common. As 2005 began, Ray's growing career began to move from the basic-cable world of the Food Network out into the mainstream and even greater popularity.

Just Say "Yum-O"

Rachael Ray's career was going great guns in 2005, exceeding even her wildest expectations. (It is interesting to note that, when Ray and her mother were assembling the recipes for her first cookbook, Elsa asked her daughter where, if the book took off, she saw herself in five years. Ray said that she would love to be on *The Oprah Winfrey Show* and would love to work for the Food Network. Sometimes it seems, dreams not only come true, but can be topped a hundredfold.) Ray had four programs in regular rotation on the Food Network: *30-Minute Meals*, *$40 a Day*, *Tasty Travels*, and *Inside Dish*. She was the network's top host, with nearly 18 million viewers tuning in to see her during the course of a week. She had taped hundreds of television shows; she had endorsed her own line of home kitchen products; and she had published 11 books, including five No. 1 best sellers. What worlds could possibly be left to conquer?

2005 turned out to be one more extraordinarily busy year for Ray, one of personal highs and lows. It was, of course, the year that she and John Cusimano were finally married in a fairy-tale wedding in Italy. The year, though, started off sadly when, in January, Boo, the beloved pit bull she had had for 12 years, suddenly died. Ray was naturally heartbroken, but months later, she and Cusimano brought a new dog into their lives, another pit bull, which they named "Isaboo."

She spent much of the year traveling, shooting segments of her show *Tasty Travels*, which premiered on August 26, 2005, as well as shooting *30-Minute Meals* back home in New York City. If that was not enough, 2005 also saw the publication of two cookbooks, *Rachael Ray's 30-Minute Get Real Meals: Eat Healthy Without Going to Extremes* and *Rachael Ray's 365: No Repeats—A Year of Deliciously Different Dinners*. That last cookbook, which took the 30-Minute Meal concept and provided the reader with one new recipe for each day of the year, was one of the most difficult projects she had had to date. "That was the stupidest idea I ever had," Ray told *The New York Times*. "That many recipes nearly killed me."[1]

Still, she wasn't done, not by a long shot. 2005 would also see Ray taking a chance on an idea whose success or failure would entirely rest on her name and the loyalty of her fans.

EVERY DAY WITH RACHAEL RAY

Magazines, not unlike talk shows, come and go. Most are failures—in a world flooded with every conceivable magazine covering every conceivable subject, it takes something special, something extra—a star—to make yet another food,

On top of her four Food Network shows, Rachael Ray tried a new endeavor in 2005—magazine publishing. Here, she promotes her new magazine, *Every Day with Rachael Ray*, in New York City. Ray wanted her magazine to provide information its readers could use.

travel and style magazine stand out from the crowd. If any-one could make a "lifestyle" magazine a success, it would be Ray. "I want to see legitimately useful information: Here are shoes you can cook in and party in," she explained to *The New York Times*. "This is more about customer service. I grew up working in resort-town restaurants. In my mind I'm a waitress. I want to give the people what they want."[2]

Unlike many other celebrities with magazines, Ray was not just going to be the name and photo on the magazine's cover. She was going to make certain that readers got what they wanted. As she told *Reader's Digest*, "The magazine is where it will all come together, everything I've been working toward for the past four years."[3] She was involved in every aspect of each issue, making sure that the magazine provided the message she hoped it would send: You don't have to be rich to have a rich life. You don't have to be rich to travel or to have adventures. Once again, Ray was taking the lessons learned from her mother and passing them on to the world.

Like everything else that Ray touched, the magazine was a huge success. *Reader's Digest*, which published the magazine, had predicted sales for the first issue of 300,000 copies. Instead, as was the case with her first cookbook, the

IN HER OWN WORDS

On her TV shows, in her books, and in her magazine, Rachael Ray aims to show that the good life is possible. She wrote about that idea in "My Journey to the Top" in *Newsweek*:

> I am sharing the idea that just learning how to make a few simple dishes for yourself or with your kids or for your friends or your lover or your brother or your cousin or your neighbor not only improves the quality of your life, it improves the quality of the lives of those you choose to share the food with. It just does. It's one of the easiest ways for a poor person to feel rich. Make good food.

first issue was a complete sellout, forcing the publishers to return to press three more times. That first issue ended up selling more than one million copies, proving that Ray's fans trusted her enough to follow her into the world of magazine publishing. By 2007, the magazine had a circulation of 1.3 million, making it one of the fastest-growing publications in the country. It was yet another success for Ray, but, unbelievably, there was one more success to come.

FROM VEGETABLES TO PEOPLE

With the successful launch of *Every Day with Rachael Ray*, it was time for both Ray and interested outside parties to begin to contemplate the next step in her career. The goal was to expand Ray's "brand" beyond the relatively limited audience of the Food Network. One way to do that would be with a daytime talk show. Before the first episode of *Rachael Ray* had been shot, some of the biggest names in show business had gotten together to make it a reality.

It was a seven-year-old girl who brought Ray to the attention of Terry Wood, the president of creative affairs and development for CBS Television Distribution. Wood had come home from work and found her daughter watching Ray on *30-Minute Meals*. Not only was she watching her, but she also knew every show that Ray was on. Wood was intrigued and asked her daughter why she liked Ray. "She said, 'I just like her right here,' and she was pointing to the frame of her face," Wood told *Vanity Fair*. "I thought, if she can drag a seven-year-old to the set, the possibilities must be endless."[4]

At the same time, Ray came to the attention of Roger King of King World Productions (now part of CBS Television Distribution) and King World's biggest star— Oprah Winfrey, who both agreed that Ray was a natural for daytime television. Meetings were held, contracts were negotiated, and when everything was hammered out, it was announced that Ray would be hosting her own syndicated daytime talk show, to be co-produced by King World, Harpo Productions (Oprah Winfrey's production company), Scripps Networks (the owners of the Food Network), and Watch Entertainment (Ray and Cusimano's production company). With such heavy hitters behind it and with Ray as the star, there was little doubt in the minds of most observers that the show would be successful.

Which is not to say that putting the show together was easy; testing out what worked for Ray would take months of time and effort. Five pilots, or "test shows," were shot before a final format and set were decided upon. Despite the changes made as testing progressed, the idea behind the show never changed. Ray wanted a show that would allow her audience to participate. She wanted to give them a forum, a chance to let their voices be heard. She told Larry King that "the number one goal of everything I do or am involved in is, Can people watch it and picture themselves doing it, trying it, living it easily?"[5]

In between tapings of her Food Network shows, work on her magazine, and preparations for her new talk show, Ray had one more major event—one that to her was perhaps the biggest honor of all. *Time* magazine had named her as one of the 100 people "who shape our world." For the little girl from Lake Luzerne, New York, it was an overwhelming honor. Ray, the woman who continually says that she has been grossly unqualified for any job she's ever held, found the whole idea unbelievable. "I just showed them how to make some easy restaurant food," she told *Biography*. "I find it ridiculous that I made that list."[6]

In her own way, though, she *has* had a huge influence over the course of her short career. As Mario Batali pointed out in *Time*, with her 30-Minute Meals, "she has radically changed the way America cooks dinner."[7] Still, Ray found the whole idea, and the dinner for the honorees, a slightly surreal experience, telling *Biography* that:

> I felt like I was going to trip on my dress and do something really stupid at any moment—somehow knock the water over the table all over the president of so and so or the Nobel Prize winner over there, you know? It was a jaw-dropping, once-in-a-lifetime, could-not-believe-I-was-there experience.[8]

After the honors and celebration were over, Ray had to get back to work. The first episode of her talk show was taped on September 7, 2006. Ray, who had never shot a show in front of a live audience before, was very nervous. She acknowledged how new the format was to her when introducing herself to her audience, saying that "for five years I've been on Food Network, national television, talking to vegetables."[9]

In fact, she was so nervous that first day of taping that, like on the first day of shooting *30-Minute Meals* when she cut off the tip of her finger, she cut deeply into the cuticle of her finger while reaching for a whisk. Ray, though, just took it in stride, considering it a stroke of good luck. (Ray takes all of her on- and off-air mishaps in extreme good humor. In an interview with *Entertainment Weekly*, she gleefully pointed out that "I am all of the most embarrassing Food Network moments in one person. My first birthday at Food Network, I was taping, and they brought me out this big cake and I leaned in and I totally Michael Jackson'd myself. I set both sides of my hair on fire. At the same time. With my own birthday candles. I am a train wreck."[10])

Despite a bad case of nerves and a bleeding cuticle, the first day went well. As did the second and the third. Ray was happy with the way the show was going, the show was a smash hit, and soon more than 100,000 people were on the waiting list to get tickets to watch a taping. It was another

A few days before her new talk show's debut, Rachael Ray taped a segment for the program. The show, though, was mainly shot before a live audience—a new feature for Ray, who joked on her first episode that she had spent her TV career before then "talking to vegetables."

certified success for Ray, who was taping 285 episodes a year of her various TV shows, writing her cookbooks, doing charity work, and trying to have a personal life as well. How does she do it?

Brooke Johnson, the president of the Food Network, advanced her own belief on *Biography*, saying that "I don't think Rachael Ray sleeps. That's my theory. I don't live in her house, but I'm pretty sure I'm right about this."[11] In truth, Ray claims she sleeps only four hours a night. "If I go to bed before 1 or 2, I'll wake up at 4 and catch an old movie until sunrise," she told *Time* magazine.[12]

Still, Ray's own mother worries that she is not getting enough rest and that she does not take good care of herself. For Ray, though, her only major health concern is keeping her voice intact. With so much talking to be done, often taping three or four shows a day, depending on what show she is doing at the time, it's easy for her to blow out her vocal cords. This is sometimes apparent on her talk show, where her voice, normally husky, on occasion becomes almost a croak.

While Ray may be concerned about her voice, one thing she has never been concerned about is her diet. While many television celebrities believe being slim is a top priority, Ray could not care less. For her, living the life she wants to live is *her* top priority, as she told *Good Housekeeping*:

> I look at dresses and jeans like any other girl and wish I could fit into them and promise myself I'll try and go to the gym. But basically, I go there maybe once a month. I could never really get so wrapped up in my own vanity that being a Size 2 would be more important than enjoying my life. And a large part of enjoying my life is great wine and great food. Those Size 0 girls sacrifice. If someone is a Size 0, they're not having a lot of fun in my book.[13]

Although comments about her weight do not bother her, other comments and stories did. As Ray's fame grew, so did her appeal to the supermarket tabloid newspapers. By the time her talk show debuted, Ray was a mainstay cover girl, as the papers vied with one another to report stories of Rachael's and John's affairs and of their pending divorce.

The problem was, of course, that none of the stories were true. But famous faces sell these newspapers, and there is a strong tendency in the tabloids to try to knock people down as soon as they become stars. When Ray first saw the kinds of stories that the tabloids were running about her and her husband, she was naturally upset. Still seeing herself as a waitress from upstate New York, she found it hard to understand that she was truly famous enough and that people were interested enough in *her* to buy tabloids with her on the cover.

Eventually, though, she learned to take it in stride, accepting it as part of the price paid for being famous. She even became able to see the humor in some of the stories. For example, one week when a particular tabloid had a cover screaming that Ray and Cusimano were filing for divorce, the couple were in Montalcino, Italy, celebrating their wedding anniversary. (They return to Montalcino every year to celebrate their anniversary. On their wedding day, they planted a tree to commemorate the occasion, and they make an annual pilgrimage back to see how "their" tree is doing.)

THE LIFE OF THE FAMOUS

Rachael Ray has become one of the most famous and trusted people in the country (ranked No. 2 after Tom Hanks, according to *Fortune* magazine), as well as head of a growing empire that has made her enormously wealthy. But she does not live the typical life of a media star. Generally shunning the limelight, she really does not like to go out. She does not enjoy going to fancy restaurants, or going to parties.

So what's a typical night like for Ray? As it turns out, it's pretty much like the life she was leading before she became famous. If she has her way, and her schedule permits, she likes to go home after work, open a bottle of wine, put on some music, and watch *Law and Order: Criminal Intent* while making dinner for her and Cusimano. Luckily for her, that's the way Cusimano prefers to spend his evenings as well. (What they don't watch on TV are any of Ray's shows. She has declared her home a "Rachael-free zone," for a number of reasons. One, she thinks that her television voice scares her dog, Isaboo. And two, she feels that, if she starts to watch herself on television, she will begin to obsess about how she looks on television, and she does not want to start doing that. Cusimano is also barred from watching his wife on television, but he admits to catching an occasional peek when she's not around.)

But it is lucky for Cusimano that, no matter how long her day has been, Ray still wants to come home and cook dinner. He said on *Chefography*, "Believe it or not, even after making 17 meals a day of *30-Minute Meals* or whatever it is, to unwind, she likes to come home and cook. Everything Rachael cooks is just out of this world—I'm the luckiest stomach on the planet."[14]

If the two of them are lucky people, they also believe in sharing their fortune with others who may not be so fortunate. In 2007, Rachael announced the formation of The Yum-o! Organization, created to help children eat healthier at home and in school. The group will work with schools to help improve the quality of cafeteria food, create scholarships, help teach parents how to feed their children healthy food, and fund charitable groups that feed needy children.

The Yum-O! Organization, which has teamed up with President Bill Clinton's Alliance for a Healthier Generation, is doing work that is near and dear to Ray's heart. Not only has she put close to $1 million of her own money into the organization and promises to spend as much as is necessary, she gives generously of her time as well. She speaks out, uses her talk show as a forum, and uses her contacts to influence the food industry to make the changes necessary to help children eat healthier. For Ray, the organization is just another aspect of the work she has always done. "It's the reason I do 30-Minute Meals," she told The Associated Press. "It's been the center vibe of everything I've ever done in my own life, simplifying good food and leading people to the good life, whether they're have-nots or haves."[15]

WHAT'S NEXT?

With television shows to shoot, cookbooks to write, a magazine to oversee, and a charitable organization to run, Ray's plate is pretty full. Could it be any fuller? Are there any new projects in the offing? And one question that many ask: Are she and Cusimano ever going to have children?

CHEFS AND CHARITY

Rachael Ray is not alone in her dedication to helping young people of all income levels have access to healthier, more nutritious food. Other chefs around the world have long been committed to giving back to the community, and especially to the young.

One of the most prominent is legendary Bay Area chef Alice Waters. As the founder and co-owner of Chez Panisse in Berkeley, California, Waters has been a longtime champion of using seasonal, locally grown fresh ingredients, and is credited with creating and developing what has become known as California Cuisine. Her impact on America's food revolution cannot be underestimated.

Waters's influence has spread far beyond her restaurant and cookbooks and into the public-school classroom. Through her Edible Schoolyard Program at Martin Luther King Jr. Middle School in Berkeley, California, she has provided urban public-school students with a one-acre organic garden to work in, along with a kitchen classroom. The program teaches young people how to grow, harvest, and prepare healthy seasonal cuisine. By showing students the connection between what they eat and where it comes from, they also become more aware of the environment and their place in it.

For the time being, despite the couple's love of children, there are no plans for kids of their own. The reason? "I don't have time," Ray told *People* magazine. "I work too much to be an appropriate parent. I feel like a bad mom to my dog some days because I'm just not here enough. I feel like I would do a bad job if I took the time to literally

On the other side of the Atlantic, popular chef and television personality Jamie Oliver has done his part as well. In 2005, he launched a campaign in Great Britain to replace unhealthy, processed foods from school lunches with nutritious food. This program faced rigorous opposition from the start: students and parents revolted, as meals of junk food were replaced with healthy meals containing two servings of fruit and three of vegetables. As time passed, though, and the students became more accustomed to the healthier food, the rebellion faded, and the program is now considered a huge success. (Oliver wants to expand the program to the United States as well.)

Along with his school lunch program, Oliver has worked to make it possible for lower-income students to become trained chefs. He recruited 15 unemployed young people, some homeless, some with learning disabilities, trained them to become professional-level chefs, and opened a restaurant in London named Fifteen for them to run. The training program and restaurant were so successful that it has now grown to four restaurants, including sites in the Netherlands and Australia, with plans to continue expanding worldwide.

Thanks to chefs like Alice Waters, Jamie Oliver, and Rachael Ray, young people throughout the world are learning the joy of eating and preparing tasty, nutritious food.

give birth to a kid right now and juggle everything I'm doing."[16]

Indeed, it sometimes seems that Ray's time is spread too thin. Reports began to surface in late 2007 and early 2008 about problems with her magazine, *Every Day with Rachael Ray*. While sales have remained strong, the magazine's rate of growth has slowed, there has been turnover among executives, and some have said that Ray has been less and less involved, as demands on her time have grown. It had become apparent that something would have to change.

So, when Ray's contract with the Food Network came up at the end of December 2007, changes *were* made. While she agreed to film 13 episodes of a new prime-time travel show, called *Rachael's Vacation*, she cut down on the number of episodes of *30-Minute Meals* shot in a year, from 80 episodes to just 60.

Even though she was going to be working less for Food Network, Ray had completely changed its programming in her short time there. Trained restaurant chefs like Mario Batali and Sara Moulton were no longer taping new cooking shows. Instead, shows like *Semi-Homemade with Sandra Lee* and *Paula's Home Cooking* (with Paula Deen) were now the rule, demonstrating simple, easy-to-make recipes, and using store-bought and prepackaged ingredients to make cooking faster and easier. Batali acknowledged the changes, telling *The New York Times*, "They don't need me. They have decided they are mass market, and they are going after the Wal-Mart crowd. [It was] a smart business decision. So they don't need someone [like me] who uses polysyllabic words from other languages."[17]

Rachael Ray has come a long way. Since debuting on the Food Network in 2001, she has changed the way America cooked, started a successful magazine, endorsed and created a popular line of cookware, married the man of her dreams, and become one of the country's most watched daytime talk

At the 2008 Daytime Emmy Awards, Rachael Ray accepts the award for Outstanding Talk Show. Holding the Emmy is the show's executive producer, Janet Annino. Ray, the small-town girl who grew up in restaurants, was living her dreams.

show hosts. And in 2008, *Rachael Ray* won a Daytime Emmy as Outstanding Talk Show. Not bad at all for a small-town girl with no professional culinary training. Taking the lessons given to her by her mother and her grandfather, she has helped Americans get over their fear of cooking, taught them that anyone has time to prepare a good meal, and brought the results of America's food revolution into households throughout the country. At only 40 years old, she still has a bright future ahead of her.

As Bob Tuschman of the Food Network said, "I cannot even predict what the future can hold for her in five years. I think this is just the beginning of people knowing who Rachael really is and what she's capable of."[18] And as long as America remains interested, it seems likely that Rachael Ray will continue to surprise, influence, educate, and entertain us.

CHRONOLOGY

1968   **August 25** Born Rachael Domenica Ray on Cape Cod, Massachusetts.

Mid-1970s   Rachael and her family move to Lake Luzerne, New York.

1986   Graduates from Lake George High School.

1991   Gets a job working at the candy counter at Macy's Marketplace; is soon promoted to manage the fresh foods department.

1993   Becomes the store manager and buyer for Agata & Valentina, a prestigious gourmet market in New York City.

1995   Becomes a food buyer for Cowan & Lobel, a gourmet market in Albany, New York; she had moved back to upstate New York after being mugged twice in less than two weeks near her apartment in Queens.

1996   Begins teaching 30-Minute Meal classes at Cowan & Lobel.

1997   Starts to do a weekly "30-Minute Meal" segment on the evening news of WRGB in Albany, winning two local Emmy awards.

1998   **December** Her first book of recipes, *30-Minute Meals*, is published.

2001   Makes a last-minute appearance on the *Today* show; meets with executives at the Food Network.

November 2 *30-Minute Meals* debuts on the Food Network.

2002   April 22 *$40 a Day* premieres on the Food Network.

        The original *30-Minute Meals* book hits *USA Today*'s best-selling books list, peaking at No. 38.

2004   Signs a multi-book deal with Clarkson Potter.

2005   September 24 Marries John Cusimano in Tuscany, Italy.

        Her magazine, *Every Day with Rachael Ray*, hits the newsstands.

2006   May *Time* magazine names her one of the "100 People Who Shape Our World."

        September Her daytime talk show, *Rachael Ray*, has its premiere.

2007   Launches the Yum-O! Organization, geared to improving children's eating habits.

        EVOO, her term for extra-virgin olive oil, is added to the *Oxford American College Dictionary*.

2008   *Rachael Ray* wins a Daytime Emmy award for Outstanding Talk Show.

NOTES

CHAPTER 1: TALKING HER WAY TO THE TOP

1. Laura Fries, "Rachael Ray," *Variety*. September 18, 2006. Available online at http://www.variety.com/review/VE1117931626.html?categoryid=32&cs=1&p=0.

2. Alessandra Stanley, "Beyond the Kitchen, Breaking Bread with America," *New York Times*. September 19, 2006. Available online at http://www.nytimes.com/2006/09/19/arts/television/19stan.html.

3. Richard Johnson, "Rachael's Dunkin' Gig 'Evil,'" *New York Post*. October 11, 2007. Available online at http://www.ny-post.com/seven/10112007/gossip/pagesix/rachaels_dunkin_gig_evil.htm.

4. Jill Hunter Pellettieri, "Rachael Ray: Why Food Snobs Should Quit Picking on Her," Slate.com. July 13, 2005. Available online at http://www.slate.com/id/2122085.

5. Ibid.

6. Mario Batali, "Rachael Ray," *Time*. April 30, 2006. Available online at http://www.time.com/time/magazine/article/0,9171,1187293,00.html.

7. Larry King, "Interview with Rachael Ray," CNN. September 18, 2006. Available online at http://transcripts.cnn.com/TRANSCRIPTS/0609/18/lkl.01.html.

8. David Carr, "Rachael Ray Gives the Gift of Time," *New York Times*. October 23, 2006. Available online at http://www.nytimes.com/2006/10/23/business/media/23carr.html?partner=rssnyt&emc=rss.

CHAPTER 2: A FOOD REVOLUTION

1. David Kamp, *The United States of Arugula: How We Became a Gourmet Nation*. New York: Broadway Books, 2006, p. 3.

2. Ibid., p. 3.

3. Ibid., p. 69.

4. Ibid., p 51.

5. Ibid., p. 87

6. Ibid., p. 90

7. Ibid., p. 70

8.   Frank Bruni, "Southwestern Sun, Late in the Day," *New York Times*. January 23, 2008. Available online at http://events.ny-times.com/2008/01/23/dining/reviews/23rest.html.

CHAPTER 3: GROWING UP WITH FOOD

1.   King. "Interview with Rachael Ray."

2.   Beverly Keel, "Rachael Ray's Recipe for Success," *AmericanProfile.com*. January 4, 2008. Available online at http://www.americanprofile.com/article/4962.html.

3.   Madeleine Marr, "30 Minutes with Food Star Rachael Ray," Knight Ridder Newspapers. March 9, 2005. Available online at http://archive.seacoastonline.com/2005news/03092005/it/68889.htm.

4.   Joanne Kaufman, "Rachael Ray's Recipe for Joy," *Good House-keeping*. August 2006.

5.   Ibid.

6.   Paul Chi, "Rachael Ray: 'I Sat Alone' in the Cafeteria," *People*. December 7, 2007. Available online at http://www.people.com/people/article/0,,20164849.00.html.

7.   Laura Jacobs, "Just Say Yum-O!" *Vanity Fair*. September 11, 2007. Available online at http://www.vanityfair.com/fame/features/2007/10/rachaelray200710.

8.   "Rachael Ray: Food Network's Waitress-Turned-Foodie Answers Our Questions," *Budget Travel*. August 1, 2005. Available online at http://www.budgettravel.com/bt-dyn/content/article/2005/08/01/AR2005080100635.html.

9.   Jacobs. "Just Say Yum-O!"

10.   Sharon Pian Chan, "TV Chef Rachael Ray Knows What It's Like to Be You," *Seattle Times*. December 21, 2005. Available online at http://seattletimes/nwsource.com/html/television/2002694780_ray21.html.

11.   Kaufman, "Recipe for Joy."

12.   Ibid.

13.   Rachael Ray, "My Journey to the Top," *Newsweek*. October 9, 2007. Available online at http://www.newsweek.com/id/42501/output/print.

14.   Keel, "Recipe for Success."

15. Lisa McKinnon, "The Anti-Martha," *Ventura County Star.* July 16, 2003. Available online at http://www.venturacountystar.com/news/2003/jul/16/the-anti-martha.

16. Keel, "Recipe for Success."

17. Kaufman, "Recipe for Joy."

18. Bob Spitz, "Rachael Ray's Secret Ingredient," *Reader's Digest.* November 2005. Available online at http://www.rd.com/rachael-rays-growing-popularity/article28697.html.

19. Jacobs, "Just Say Yum-O!"

20. Kaufman, "Recipe for Joy."

21. Jacobs, "Just Say Yum-O!"

22. "Rachael Ray," *Chefography.* Food Network, Episode CHSP09.

CHAPTER 4: LIFE IN THE BIG CITY

1. Jacobs, "Just Say Yum-O!"

2. "Rachael Ray Bio," *Every Day with Rachael Ray* Web site. Available online at http://www.rachaelraymag.com/about-rachael/rachael-ray-biography/article.html.

3. Mimi Sheraton, "Marketplace for the Evolving Gourmets," *New York Times.* January 18, 1977.

4. Ibid.

5. Jacobs, "Just Say Yum-O!"

6. "Rachael Ray," *Chefography.*

7. Ibid.

8. Kim Severson, "Being Rachael Ray: How Cool Is That," *New York Times.* October 19, 2005. Available online at http://nytimes.com/2005/10/19/dining/19rach.html.

9. "Rachael Ray," *Chefography.*

10. Ibid.

11. Jacobs, "Just Say Yum-O!"

12 Ibid.

13. "Rachael Ray," *Chefography.*

CHAPTER 5: BIRTH OF THE 30-MINUTE MEAL

1. Ibid.

2. Ibid.

3. Rachael Ray, *30-Minute Meals*. New York: Lake Isle Press, 1998, p. 130.

4. Jacobs, "Just Say Yum-O!"

5. Ibid.

6. Keel, "Recipe for Success."

7. "Rachael Ray," *Chefography*.

8. Rachael Ray, "My Journey to the Top."

9. "Rachael Ray," *Chefography*.

10. Jacobs, "Just Say Yum-O!"

11. "Rachael Ray," *Chefography*.

12. Kaufman, "Recipe for Joy," p. 119.

13. "Rachael Ray," *Chefography*.

14. Ray, "My Journey to the Top."

15. Severson, "Being Rachael Ray."

CHAPTER 6: A FOOD NETWORK STAR IS BORN

1. Karu F. Daniels, "Rachael Ray: Developing Story," *Black Voices* Web site. May 1, 2007. Available online at http://www.blackvoices.com/blogs/2007/05/01/rachael-ray-story-developing.

2. "Rachael Ray," *Chefography*.

3. Ibid.

4. "Rachael Ray," *Biography*. The Biography Channel.

5. Ibid.

6. Jacobs, "Just Say Yum-O!"

7. "Rachael Ray," *Chefography*.

8. Jacobs, "Just Say Yum-O!"

9. Ibid.

10. "Rachael Ray," *Chefography*.

11. Jacobs, "Just Say Yum-O!"

12. Daniels, "Rachael Ray: Developing Story."

13. King, "Interview with Rachael Ray."

14. "Rachael Ray," *Chefography*.

15. Jacobs, "Just Say Yum-O!"

16. "Rachael Ray Can't Stop Talking," *Redbook*. October 2006. Available online at http://www.redbookmag.com/your/rachael-ray-interview=yl.

CHAPTER 7: SHE NEVER STOPS

1. Ibid.
2. Ibid.
3. "Rachael Ray," *Biography*.
4. King, "Interview with Rachael Ray."
5. Ibid.
6. Ibid.
7. Ibid.
8. Ibid.
9. Marr, "30 Minutes with Food Star Rachael Ray."
10. "Rachael Ray," *Biography*.
11. Ibid.
12. Liza Hamm and Michelle Tauber, "Rachael Ray's Recipe for Marriage," *People*. May 2, 2007. Available online at http://www.people.com/people/article/0,,20037511,00.html.
13. Ibid.
14. Kaufman, "Recipe for Joy."
15. "Rachael Ray," *Chefography*.
16. Severson, "Being Rachael Ray."
17. Keel, "Recipe for Success."
18. "Rachael Ray," *Biography*.
19. Ibid.
20. Severson, "Being Rachael Ray."
21. Ibid.
22. Jacobs, "Just Say Yum-O!"
23. Ibid.
24. Pellettieri, "Rachael Ray: Why Food Snobs Should Quit Picking on Her."
25. Severson, "Being Rachael Ray."
26. Jacobs, "Just Say Yum-O!"
27. Severson, "Being Rachael Ray."
28. King, "Interview with Rachael Ray."

CHAPTER 8: JUST SAY "YUM-O"

1. Severson, "Being Rachael Ray."

2. Lia Miller, "From Food Network to the Magazine Rack," *New York Times*. April 25, 2005. Available online at http://www.nytimes.com/2005/04/25/business/media/25readersdigest.html.

3. Spitz, "Rachael Ray's Secret Ingredient."

4. Jacobs, "Just Say Yum-O!"

5. King, "Interview with Rachael Ray."

6. "Rachael Ray," *Biography*.

7. Batali, "Rachael Ray."

8. "Rachael Ray," *Biography*.

9. King, "Interview with Rachael Ray."

10. Dan Snierson, "Stupid Questions with Rachael Ray," *Entertainment Weekly*. October 13, 2006. Available online at http://www.ew.com/article/0,,1545622,00.html.

11. "Rachael Ray," *Biography*.

12. Joel Stein, "Rachael Ray Has a Lot on Her Plate," *Time*. September 5, 2006. Available online at http://www.time.com/time/magazine/article/0.9171,1531337,00.html.

13. Kaufman, "Recipe for Joy."

14. "Rachael Ray," *Chefography*.

15. J.M. Hirsch, "Rachael Ray Launches Charity and Teams with Bill Clinton to Get Kids Eating Healthier," *North County Times*. April 25, 2007. Available online at www.nctimes.com/articles/2007/04/25/food/16_11_054_25_07.txt.

16. Hamm and Tauber, "Rachael Ray's Recipe for Marriage."

17. Elizabeth Jensen, "Changing Courses at the Food Network." *New York Times*. December 17, 2007. Available online at http://www.nytimes.com/2007/12/17/business/media/17food.html.

18. "Rachael Ray," *Biography*.

BIBLIOGRAPHY

Batali, Mario. "Rachael Ray." *Time*, April 30, 2006. Available online at http://www.time.com/time/magazine/article/0,9171,1187293,00.html.

Benson, Jim. "Rachael Ray Rules in Ratings." *Broadcasting & Cable*, October 3, 2006. Available online at http://www.broadcastingcable.com/article/CA6377767.html.

Bruni, Frank. "Southwestern Sun, Late in the Day." *New York Times*, January 23, 2008. Available online at http://events.nytimes.com/2008/01/23/dining/reviews/23rest.html.

Carr, David. "Rachael Ray Gives the Gift of Time." *New York Times*, October 23, 2006. Available online at http://www.nytimes.com/2006/10/23/business/media/23carr.html?partner=rssnyt&emc=rss.

Chan, Sharon Pian. "TV Chef Rachael Ray Knows What It's Like to Be You." *Seattle Times*, December 21, 2005. Available online at http://seattletimes.nwsource.com/html/television/2002694780_ray21.html.

Chi, Paul. "Rachael Ray: 'I Sat Alone' in the Cafeteria." *People*, December 7, 2007. Available online at http://www.people.com/people/article/0,,2016489,00.html.

Cohn, Angel. "Rachael Ray Cooks Up Saucy Dish." *AOL Television*. Available online at http://television.aol.com/tv-celebrity-interviews/rachael-ray.

Daniels, Karu F. "Rachael Ray: Developing Story." *Black Voices* Web site. May 1, 2007. Available online at http://www.blackvoices.com/blogs/2007/05/01/rachael-ray-story-developing.

"*Every Day with Rachael Ray* Has a New Publisher." *FishbowlNY*. November 7, 2007. Available online at http://www.mediabistro.com/fishbowlny/the_revolving_door/balaban_named_every_day_publisher.705.

Finn, Natalie. "Rachael Ray Timeline: A Media Star Is Born." *Television Week*, January 15, 2007. Available online at http://goliath.ecnext.com.

Fries, Laura. "Rachael Ray." *Variety*, September 18, 2006. Available online at http://www.variety.com/review/VE1117931626.html?categoryid=32&cs=1&p=0.

Hamm, Liza, and Michelle Tauber. "Rachael Ray's Recipe for Marriage." *People*, May 2, 2007. Available online at http://www.people.com/people/article/0,,20037511,00.html.

Hazan, Marcella. *Essentials of Classic Italian Cooking*. New York: Alfred A. Knopf, 1992.

Hirsch, J.M. "Rachael Ray Launches Charity and Teams with Bill Clinton to Get Kids Eating Healthier." *North County Times*, April 25, 2007. Available online at http://www.nctimes.com/articles/2007/04/25/food/16_11_054_25_07.txt.

Hixson, David L. "Daytime Talk Shows." *St. James Encyclopedia of Pop Culture*. Available online at http://findarticles.com/p/articles/mi_g1epc/is_tov/ai_2419100327.

Jacobs, Laura. "Just Say Yum-O!' *Vanity Fair*, September 11, 2007. Available online at http://www.vanityfair.com/fame/features/2007/10/rachaelray200710.

Jensen, Elizabeth. "Changing Courses at the Food Network." *New York Times*, December 17, 2007. Available online at http://www.nytimes.com/2007/12/17/business/media/17food.html.

Johnson, Richard. "Rachael's Dunkin' Gig 'Evil.'" *New York Post*. October 11, 2007. Available online at http://www.nypost.com/seven/10112007/gossip/pagesix/rachaels_dunkin_gig_evil.htm.

Kamp, David. *The United States of Arugula: How We Became a Gourmet Nation*. New York: Broadway Books, 2006.

Kaufman, Joanne. "Rachael Ray's Recipe for Joy." *Good Housekeeping*, August 2006.

Keel, Beverly. "Rachael Ray's Recipe for Success." *AmericanProfile.com*. January 4, 2008. Available online at http://www.americanprofile.com/article/4692.html.

Kelly, Keith J. "No Days With Ray." *New York Post*, January 16, 2008. Available online at http://www.nypost.com/seven/01162008/business/no_days_with_ray_816024.htm.

Kelly, Keith J. "Ray's Pizzazz Fades." *New York Post*, October 3, 2007. Available online at http://www.nypost.com/seven/10032007/business/rays_pizzazz_fades.htm.

King, Larry. "Interview with Rachael Ray." CNN, September 18, 2006. Available online at http://transcripts.cnn.com/TRANSCRIPTS/0609/18/lkl.01.html.

Marr, Madeleine. "30 Minutes with Food Star Rachael Ray." Knight Ridder Newspapers. March 9, 2005. Available online at http://archive.seacostonline.com/2005news/03092005/it/68889.htm.

McKinnon, Lisa. "The Anti-Martha." *Ventura County Star*. July 16, 2003. Available online at http://www.venturacountystar.com/news/2003/jul/16/the-anti-martha.

"Meet Rachael Ray." *Food Network* Web site. Available online at http://www.foodnetwork.com/food/rachael_ray/0,1974,FOOD_9928,00.html.

Miller, Lia. "From Food Network to the Magazine Rack." *New York Times*. April 25, 2005. Available online at http://www.nytimes.com/2005/04/25/business/media/25readersdigest.html.

Moore, Brett. "Rachael Ray." About.com. Available online at http://gourmetfood.about.com/od/chefbiographie1/p/rachaelraybio.htm.

Pellettieri, Jill Hunter, "Rachael Ray: Why Food Snobs Should Quit Picking on Her." *Slate*. July 13, 2005. Available online at www.slate.com/id/2122085/.

"Pop Crazy Interviews the Food Network's Numbers Girl." Available online at http://www.popcrazy.com/features/rachaelray.php.

"Rachael-isms." *Every Day with Rachael Ray* Web site. Available online at http://www.rachaelraymag.com/about-rachael/rachael-isms/article.html.

"Rachael Ray Bio." *Every Day with Rachael Ray* Web site. Available online at http://www.rachaelraymag.com/about-rachael/rachael-ray-biography/article.html.

"Rachael Ray." Available online at http://www.hwwilson.com/_home/bios/20031113414.htm.

"Rachael Ray." *Biography*. The Biography Channel.

"Rachael Ray Can't Stop Talking," *Redbook*. October 2006. Available online at http://www.redbookmag.com/your/rachael-ray-interview-yl.

"Rachael Ray." *Chefography*. Food Network, Episode CHSP09.

"Rachael Ray: Food Network's Waitress-Turned-Foodie Answers Our Questions." *Budget Travel*. August 1, 2005. Available online at http://www.budgettravel.com/bt-dyn/content/article/2005/08/01/AR2005080100635.html.

Ray, Rachael. *30-Minute Meals*. New York: Lake Isle Press, 1998.

———. *Rachael Ray's 365: No Repeats—A Year of Deliciously Different Dinners*. New York: Clarkson Potter, 2005.

———. "My Journey to the Top." *Newsweek*. October 9, 2007. Available online at http://www.newsweek.com/id/42501/output/print.

Rockwell, Page. "Bite Me!" *Salon.com*, June 26, 2006. Available online at http://www.salon.com/mwt/feature/2006/06/26/bourdain_QA/.

Severson, Kim, "Being Rachael Ray: How Cool Is That?" *New York Times*, October 19, 2005. Available online at http://nytimes.com/2005/10/19/dining/19rach.html.

Sheraton, Mimi. "Marketplace for the Evolving Gourmets." *New York Times*. January 18, 1977.

Snierson, Dan. "Stupid Questions with Rachael Ray." *Entertainment Weekly*, October 13, 2006. Available online at http://www.ew.com/ew/article/0,,1545622,00.html.

Spitz, Bob. "Rachael Ray's Secret Ingredient." *Reader's Digest*, November 2005. Available online at http://www.rd.com/rachael-rays-growing-popularity/article28697.html.

Stanley, Alessandra. "Beyond the Kitchen, Breaking Bread with America." *New York Times*, September 19, 2006. Available online at http://www.nytimes.com/2006/09/19/arts/television/19stan.html.

Stein, Joel. "Rachael Ray Has a Lot on Her Plate." *Time*, September 5, 2006. Available online at http://www.time.com/time/magazine/article/0,9171,1531337,00.html.

FURTHER RESOURCES

BOOKS

Batali, Mario. *Molto Italiano: 327 Simple Italian Recipes to Cook at Home*. New York: Ecco, 2005.

Pollan, Michael. *In Defense of Food: An Eater's Manifesto*. New York: Penguin Press, 2008.

Ray, Rachael. *Comfort Food: Rachael Ray's Top 30 30-Minute Meals*. New York: Lake Isle Press, 2005.

———. *Rachael Ray's Big Orange Book*. New York: Clarkson Potter, 2008.

———. *Yum-O! The Family Cookbook*. New York: Clarkson Potter, 2008.

Waters, Alice. *The Art of Simple Food: Notes, Lessons and Recipes from a Delicious Revolution*. New York: Clarkson Potter, 2007.

WEB SITES

Every Day with Rachael Ray
http://www.rachaelraymag.com

Everything Rachael Ray
http://rachaelrayblog.blogspot.com

Food Network
http://www.foodnetwork.com

Rachael Ray
http://www.rachaelray.com

Rachael Ray: Rachael's Daytime Talk Show
http://www.rachaelrayshow.com

INDEX

ABOUT THE AUTHOR

DENNIS ABRAMS is the author of numerous books for Chelsea House, including biographies of Barbara Park, Anthony Horowitz, Victor Yushchenko, Ty Cobb, Albert Pujols, the Beastie Boys, Jay-Z, and Xerxes. He attended Antioch College, where he majored in English and communications. He currently lives in Houston, Texas, with his partner of 19 years, two cats, and a dog named Junie B.

PICTURE CREDITS